GHOSTS
WEREWOLVES
WITCHES & VAMPIRES

Jo-Anne Christensen

Illustrations by Arlana Anderson-Hale

Lone Pine Publishing

The Publisher: Lone Pine Publishing

10145 – 81 Avenue	1901 Raymond Ave. SW,
Edmonton, AB T6E 1W9	Suite C, Renton, WA 98055
Canada	USA

Website: http://www.lonepinepublishing.com

National Library of Canada Cataloguing in Publication Data

Christensen, Jo-Anne.
  Ghosts, werewolves, witches & vampires

  ISBN 1-55105-333-0

  1. Ghosts. 2. Supernatural. I. Title.
GR580.C58 2001   398.25   C2001-911199-1

Editorial Director: Nancy Foulds
Project Editor: Shelagh Kubish
Production Manager: Jody Reekie
Book Design, Layout & Production: Arlana Anderson-Hale
Cover Design: Arlana Anderson-Hale

We acknowledge the financial support of the Government of Canada
through the Book Publishing Industry Development Program (BPIDP)
for our publishing activities.

PC: P6

Dedication

For my dear friend
Barbara Smith,
who has so generously led me
into this work that I love.

Contents

Acknowledgments

Every book that I have written has come to be because of the kind and generous support of many individuals. This collection of stories is no exception, and I must pause for a moment to offer my sincere gratitude.

The management and staff of Lone Pine Publishing are always owed a mention: you are wonderful people to work with, one and all. In particular, I wish to thank Shane Kennedy and Nancy Foulds for their continued enthusiasm and support, and Shelagh Kubish for being such a talented editor and true pleasure to work with. Arlana Anderson-Hale is the wonderful artist who brought these mysterious creatures to life, and I thank her sincerely for lending her tremendous creativity to the project.

My husband, Dennis, was particularly helpful in this project, somehow managing the diametrically opposed roles of both practical advisor and creative muse. Our children, Steven, Gracie, William and Natalie, are always an inspiration and a joy. I love you all.

Finally, I must thank all the authors and movie-makers who create the wonderfully frightening, supernatural stories that I love—and the paranormal researchers who intrigue me with the idea that every one of those dark visions might be based upon something true.

Together, you captured my imagination long ago. I hope you never set it free.

Introduction

When my oldest child, Steven, was not yet two years old, he was invited to attend a children's Halloween party. I got right into the spirit of it—Halloween is one of my favorite events—and put him into a little costume with full makeup and delivered him to the festivities. When we arrived, however, I couldn't help feeling that my kid was just a little out of step. There, amidst the black and orange streamers and balloons, were a clown, several princesses and a kitty-cat. I noted an assortment of other cute, fluffy, funny, non-threatening creatures. There was only one tiny Grim Reaper, though, and that was my boy, looking as pleased as punch and desperately out of place with his ominous black hood and his tin-foil sickle.

In the end, it didn't matter. The kids all had fun and, in the four years since, no parents have come forward to accuse me of traumatizing their children on that day. For that reason, and others, I still stand by my choice of costume. After all, Halloween is not about puppies and Power Rangers. It's about the "thinning veil," the one night each year when the worlds of the living and dead overlap. For most people, it's meant to be entertaining and fun (with no disrespect intended to those who mark it as a significant religious date), and perhaps pre-schoolers should stick to cartoonish versions of the potentially frightening images, but I believe in running with the appropriate subject matter. I think there's nothing wrong with taking every October 31 to address our fear of that which is supernatural and unknown.

That fear is huge, and it is strangely exhilarating to wallow in it. When I was no more than six or seven years old, I used to beg my mother to tell me the stories of scary movies she had seen. Her rendition of *The House of Wax* gave me nightmares for a week. To this day, I've never seen the movie, but mention of it gives me chills.

They're good chills, though. And the enjoyment I got out of that story—imagining Vincent Price dipping his hapless victims in molten goo—was worth a few nightmares. I could say the same for any number of macabre comic books or creepy episodes of *The Twilight Zone* or *Night Gallery*.

In retrospect, I don't know why I was allowed to see that stuff—today, I won't even let my kids watch *The 13 Ghosts of Scooby Doo*. But, hypocritical though it may be, I'm glad that my parents weren't that conscientious. Had there been stricter rules regarding the television when I was a child, I might be in an entirely different profession.

I think it's reasonable to assume that I got to watch the scary shows because Mom and Dad wanted to watch the scary shows. So did everyone else. I remember all my friends and family members being fascinated with the paranormal, whether it came in the form of fiction or fact.

We often told true ghost stories when we got together. Everyone knew someone who had experienced a psychic moment or had a visit from a dead relative, and to relay the details of such an encounter was to command the attention of everyone present. Ouija boards were popular, too, when I was growing up in the 70s, and we all experimented at one time or another. I remember crawling into the dark space under our wooden porch with a friend and a lit candle, seeking suitably atmospheric surroundings for a midday séance. The occasion was uneventful—we failed to contact the dead and, happily, did not burn down the house—but our enchantment with the unknown continued.

In my teen years, my friends and I loved to read to one another from a well-thumbed paperback that contained lurid true stories about the White Witch of Rose Hall, the Countess Bathory and the Vampire of Dusseldorf. We delighted in the blood-soaked drama of these stories, and our fascination was intensified by the idea that each account was rooted in fact. Somehow, the knowledge that something like *The Amityville Horror* really happened got our adrenaline pumping the way no pure fiction could. (That particular story's appeal was reduced to approximately nothing, once it was debunked.)

A few years ago, I indulged my interest in the strange-but-true, and began to write collections of non-fiction ghost stories. The people I interviewed were often so credible, I found it impossible to *not* believe them. And so, my interest in the factual side of the paranormal world grew tremendously. My infatuation with moody storytelling lingered, though, and I eventually began to wonder what sort of a hybrid might result if I combined my two loves: dramatically written tales and their rooted-in-reality counterparts. Something told me that it might be fun. Something was right; it has been.

The stories you'll find in these pages are all grounded in fact. They've been written in a dramatic style, however, and are meant to be entertaining. You might compare them more to a theatrical movie that is based upon a true event than to a documentary about the same. It is just that by infusing the truth with some color, and drama, and sense of character and place, I hope to draw you in, and then make you shiver. You know—in that good way, the way that feels as though an icy, skeletal finger is tickling your spine...

In terms of subject matter, there were, of course, a multitude of creepy creatures to choose from. For this volume, however, I decided to concentrate on the scary story "classics" as it were: witches, werewolves, vampires, and ghosts.

These creatures are my favorites, so much so I think that next Halloween, I might just dress my four kids as a witch, a werewolf, a vampire and a ghost. And if any of the mermaids or duckies take issue with it, I'll just have to remind them:

Sometimes it's fun to visit the dark side.

Part One

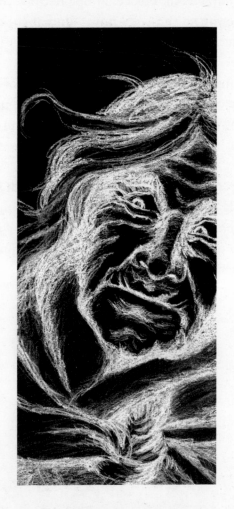

Witches

In the year 1692, in Salem, Massachusetts, four young Puritan girls spent a few winter evenings amusing themselves with fortune-telling games. The guilt and fear that they experienced when dabbling in the occult led them to eventually confess their secret—and accuse two local women and a Caribbean servant of bewitching them. Their actions unleashed a fury of superstitious paranoia. Before it died down, 150 people stood accused, and 20—those who would not confess—were executed for their diabolical crimes.

The Salem witch trials were an echo of the witch-hunting frenzy that gripped western Europe during the 15th, 16th and 17th centuries and stood as an example of the fears and superstitions that European immigrants brought with them to the new world. Three hundred years later, many of those fears have dissipated. The mention of witchcraft now inspires more curiosity than dread, and our concept of witches has broadened to include a wider variety of archetypes.

There are Wiccans, who celebrate their connectedness to nature and all things in the universe. Conversely, there are practitioners of black witchcraft, who claim to ally themselves with the devil. Somewhere in the middle fall those witches who practice traditional folk magic and medicine and who are able to use their powers to either help or harm, as they see fit.

Our collective consciousness has even expanded so much as to include the image of the beautiful, wholesome, young witch, illustrated by such television shows as Bewitched and Sabrina, The Teenage Witch. For the most part, however, popular culture still embraces the witch who is, if not menacing, at least mysterious in her ways.

Great powers we cannot understand just seem to make for a better story...

Miss Addie

Every chair in the doctor's waiting room was filled. There were people with coughs who tried to cover their mouths conscientiously, and those who sat beside them and angled their bodies just slightly away. There were people with problems that weren't obvious to others, who sat quietly and looked worried. And there were healthy-looking people, checking their watches with irritation and wondering if they should rebook their routine physical exams for another day.

Sarah was one of the apparently healthy ones. Though she was in her eighties, her slight body was spry, and her blue eyes snapped with interest. Her hair was tidily twisted into a roll, she was wearing one of her nicest cotton print dresses and, in a certain way, she looked fresher and prettier than the harried granddaughter who always escorted Sarah to her appointments.

The granddaughter's name was Joan, and she had risked leaving her chair empty for a few moments in order to speak with the receptionist who reigned over the waiting area from behind an opaque sliding glass window. Over the shuffle of magazine pages and the discreet sniffling, Sarah could hear little pieces of the hushed conversation that Joan was having.

"...it's already been an hour and a half..."

"...care to reschedule for another day?..."

"...difficult to organize the time..."

Sarah didn't mind the wait. It was pleasant to sit where she could watch so many different people and play little guessing games in her mind about the lives that each of them lived outside of the doctor's office. It was not so easy for Joan, however; she knew that. Joan was busy with a house to keep and meals to cook and three small children to care for. The youngest, Cory, had been brought along for the outing and had exhausted his two-year-old supply of patience roughly 15 minutes after they had arrived. Joan held an iron grip on one of his small hands as she exchanged terse words with the receptionist. Cory yanked on his mother's arm mercilessly, trying to get free. He finally settled for simply collapsing, so that Joan was forced to support all 35 pounds of him from one dangling limb.

The sliding window closed. Joan walked back to her seat with Cory struggling in her grasp. Her features were pinched with tension, but she tried to sound positive when she spoke to Sarah.

"Gran," she said, "it's going to be a little while longer. Are you okay waiting here for a bit more?"

Sarah smiled at her granddaughter. "I'm fine, dear. But this might be taking too much of your time, I fear."

"Oh, no. No, no. Don't worry about that," Joan assured her, but her voice sounded faraway. Sarah, who was more aware of the challenges of modern family life than anyone gave her credit for, took one look at her granddaughter's distracted expression and knew that she was forming a frantic contingency plan. Someone would have to be called so that the older children would be met when they arrived home from school. Something different would need to be arranged for dinner, something quick, because Caitlyn had soccer practice at 6:30. Sarah was sorry for Joan's troubles but could think of nothing within her power that would help. So, instead of fretting, she returned to her pleasant pastime of people watching.

"So many people for one doctor," mused Sarah, as she surveyed the crowded room. Joan, who had begun to busily bounce Cory on one of her knees, nodded.

"Well, he's a good doctor, Gran. That's why."

Sarah smiled. "I'm sure he's lovely. So was my old doctor, very nice. But when I was a girl, if we got sick or hurt, there was good care then, too. Maybe even better. And there was none of this—no waiting, no appointments, no girl in a cage..." She waved one thin, freckled hand vaguely in the direction of the glassed-in reception desk. There were friendly snickers from those people sitting close enough to hear.

"Well," said Joan, and the weariness was beginning to show in her voice. "I suppose there were fewer patients, or more doctors, or something, back then."

"Oh, we didn't bother to go to doctors so much," said Sarah.

"Who, then?"

"We went to witches."

Joan's body stiffened, and she stopped bouncing Cory. The waiting room was quiet, and although most people still appeared to be reading their well-thumbed magazines, several were wearing identical, small smiles. Joan doubted that they were being amused by the dated issues of *Time* and felt a flush rising on her face.

"Gran!" she whispered. "You did *not!*"

Sarah turned to look at her granddaughter, and was amused by her obvious embarrassment.

"Oh, yes, Joannie," Sarah spoke at full volume, ignoring her granddaughter's cue to lower her voice. "Witches were common, then. Not the pointy black hat kind, you know, but women with special powers. They could help anybody with any sort of problem. Injuries, afflictions; they could cure a person off the whiskey, take away a sunburn and, of course, help babies be born." Sarah smiled and stroked Cory's fat cheek with one gnarled finger.

"That's superstition, Gran," said Joan.

Sarah arched one thin eyebrow. "Is it?" she asked. "When I was a girl, in Balsam Grove, we had a good witch. Maybe the best one in all of North Carolina. I'll never forget her name: it was Addie Welch." Sarah's eyes took on a dreamy look as the memory took hold.

"Everyone called her Miss Addie..."

Sarah remembered Miss Addie Welch well. She was a witch, a powerful witch whose spells and potions were relied upon daily by the simple people who lived in the little mountain community. Miss Addie would be called when a child had a fever, or the milk thrush was paining its little mouth. She had remedies for rashes and burns and ways to calm an excitable temperament. She could mend a jagged cut and make the scar appear someplace where no one would see it. And by laying her cold hands on a woman's swollen belly, Miss Addie could hasten a baby into the world or keep it from coming too soon. There was no illness she could not cure, no injury she could not heal, and the folks of Balsam Grove were grateful that they had someone to whom they could turn when such misfortune threatened to unravel their generally happy lives.

Though she could never remember the witch doing anything but good, as a child, Sarah had found her frightening. Part of it was Miss Addie's appearance—with her gaunt frame wrapped in dark, heavy shawls and her strange, tawny-colored eyes, she was simply too somber looking to appeal to a little girl. But a greater part of it was the woman's mysterious power—the fact that Miss Addie could *do things* to people—and the possibility that if she didn't like you, the things that she did might be bad. The children all shared this terrible awe, and even the ones who had benefited from the witch's inscrutable abilities fell silent and wide-eyed in her presence.

When the children were not in Miss Addie's presence, they sometimes made up terrible stories about her. One girl said that Chester Wilkes had not really gone away to prison; that in fact, Miss Addie had turned him into a toad and he was living in the pond down at the bottom of the Wilkeses' barnyard. A boy named Raymond claimed to have seen Miss Addie riding a horse across his father's field at midnight, and said that everyone knew how evil witches turned lost children into horses so that they could ride them to exhaustion. Sarah's own best friend, Patsy Campbell, told her that Miss Addie was nearly 200 years old, and that she had to perform one human sacrifice under the full moon for every additional 10 years of immortality. There had been many nights when Sarah had lain in her bed, staring out the window at the roundness of the moon and wondering exactly when Miss Addie was due to offer another life for another decade.

That was the night. Usually, during the day, there was little time to be haunted by childhood fears of any form. Sarah often found herself busy in the kitchen with her mother, making sweet pickles and jam, plucking a fat chicken to put in the oven or cutting biscuits out of a rolled sheet of dough with a floury metal ring. Outside, there were always cows to be milked and hogs to be slopped and the barn to be swept clean. Sarah loved to help her parents with these chores; it made her feel proud and responsible.

The year Sarah turned 10, she was allowed to help with a very big job: the hog butchering. Her aunts and uncles had come over to work, and her younger brothers were shooed away to play at the neighbor's house. They had protested loudly that they wanted to stay, being ghoulish little boys who were desperate to witness something so terribly gory. Her parents had been insistent, though. "We can't have you underfoot," they said. "What about Sarah?" the boys screeched, deeply offended by the unfairness of it all. "Sarah is staying because she'll be a great help," the parents said, and Sarah had nearly burst from pride.

The men worked in the barn, cutting the meat on a makeshift table, a huge sheet of wood they had set upon some sawhorses. The women worked in the yard, rendering huge iron potfuls of hog fat into lard. Sarah helped tend the fire that melted the bubbling fat, adding pieces of split, dry wood when necessary.

The heavy vats had been set directly in the orange flames, carefully balanced on stacks of bricks. Sarah had just added a handful of sticks to the fire when one of the bricks crumbled under its load. The black iron pot came crashing down on its side, sending a lake of lava-hot hog fat washing over the little girl's bare feet.

The barnyard filled with screams. There were Sarah's own howls of agony, and the horrified cries that came from her mother and her aunt. The men came rushing to see what had happened and added their own shouts and curses.

Then Sarah's father scooped her up in his arms, and the chaos of the scene faded into the distance.

He ran. Later, Sarah would remember the jagged sound of his breath and the way the trees had appeared to be bouncing as she jostled about. The searing pain in her feet had eclipsed every other conscious thought, however, and she had not realized where she was being taken until her father kicked open the creaky gate to Miss Addie's yard. The witch was standing on the step, waiting, as though she had been expecting them.

"Bring her in," she said to Sarah's father, "and I'll take the fire out of her."

Sarah was placed gently on a faded sofa in Miss Addie's shadowy parlor. Her father hovered over her for a few moments, wringing his hands and looking nervous. Then the witch told him to wait in the yard, and he left.

He left—and, suddenly, Sarah was all alone with Miss Addie Welch and two tortured feet that were no good for running away.

The heavy draperies in Miss Addie's parlor had been pulled closed and tied in place with braided fabric cords. There was very little light entering the room, but as Sarah stared up at the tall, imposing figure that loomed over her, she saw the strangest glow reflecting off her solemn face. As the witch stooped over, bringing her face close to Sarah's, the girl realized that there was no reflection. The illumination was emanating from Miss Addie's strange, tawny eyes.

Sarah noticed her hands then—her big, crooked, cold witch's hands with their dirty fingernails and strange rings. Those hands were raised up; they were reaching out; the fingers were curled into claws and ready to clamp firmly around Sarah's small, white neck. Sarah tried to scream and found that her voice would not come. She thought of fighting back, but her limbs were paralyzed with fear. She imagined that, in a few minutes, Miss Addie would arrange her features in their most solemn expression and go out to the yard to tell her father, "I'm sorry, but Sarah could not be saved." He would cry, but he would suspect nothing, and her family would never know what had happened, that she had been sacrificed so that a dirty old witch could live for another 10 years.

And then, Miss Addie clamped her hands firmly over Sarah's ears.

The girl was so surprised that she tried to push herself upright on the sofa, but the old woman's strong arms kept her firmly in place. Her strange, bright eyes looked oddly unfocused, and her thin lips were moving rapidly, but Sarah could not hear a word of what was being said.

After several minutes, Miss Addie took her hands away from Sarah's ears and placed them on her peeling, blistering feet. The pain rose up like a knife to meet the witch's fingertips, and Sarah's voice came back to her. She screamed, and many years later, her father admitted to her that when he heard that piercing, pained sound, he had been forced to cover his own ears in anguish. Then, as the sound of her own agony still echoed in the small house, the pain quickly subsided, slipping away until it had completely disappeared. Sarah fell back on the cushions of the sofa, weak with relief and from the strain of the ordeal. Miss Addie touched one cool finger against Sarah's forehead, and the girl fell asleep.

When Sarah awoke, it was late evening. Her father had come to fetch her, and the lines of concern melted away from his face as he examined her feet. He started to ask Miss Addie what she had done, then remembered himself and simply thanked her. She waved the two of them away; she was busy baking bread and had no time for chitchat. As Sarah walked home on her own two feet, holding her father's hand, she carried with her the distinct impression that the woman who was measuring out flour and lard by yellow lamplight in the cluttered kitchen was not the same woman who had leaned over her injured body only hours earlier.

"That's a good story, Gran," said Joan, as she fished through her purse for something, anything, with which she could amuse Cory. She finally handed over her car keys, which pleased him immensely.

Several people in the waiting room had dropped the pretense of reading and had tossed their worn magazines back on the white plastic coffee table. They were all focused upon Sarah and smiling with interest.

"So your feet were completely healed?" asked one woman.

"Did she charge you any money?" inquired a graying man with a bandaged hand and a briefcase.

Sarah smiled sweetly at her audience.

"My feet have never bothered me a day since," she said. "About the money—I'm not sure, you know. As a child, I never thought of such things, and when I grew up and married, we moved away to the city, where there were no neighborhood witches to take care of us."

A teenage girl sat in rapt attention, her wide eyes glued to Sarah.

"That is *so* cool," she breathed.

Sarah leaned toward her and nodded solemnly.

"It *is* cool, isn't it, dear?" she said, then leaned back and added, "of course, my granddaughter doesn't believe me."

"Oh, Gran..." Joan began, flustered that Sarah's followers were suddenly focused upon her. "It's not that. It's just, I don't know...so..."

And then the nurse called Sarah's name, and Joan was saved from having to respond further.

The small examining room felt even more crowded than did the waiting room. There was the young doctor, with his white coat and stethoscope and clipboard, talking to Joan, who had Cory balanced upon one hip. Then there was Sarah, sitting primly and serenely on the paper-covered examination table, looking tiny with her thin arms and legs poking out of the wraparound gown.

"She has some trouble with her blood pressure," Joan was telling the doctor, "and a bit of a hard time with her left hip, especially when the weather's damp." She lowered her voice to a murmur, as she told him, "Her mental alertness, and her memory...I can see it slipping a little."

"Yes, but fortunately my hearing is excellent," Sarah piped cheerfully. Joan's face turned crimson, and Sarah felt a pang of guilt. She was fortunate to have a kind granddaughter who was willing to take her places, and she resolved that in the future she would mind her smart mouth.

The doctor smiled and turned to face her.

"Well, Sarah," he said. "I'd like to examine you now, if that's alright."

Sarah nodded her consent. The young fellow took her pressure, with the big cuff that wrapped so many times around her arm, and used his stethoscope to listen to her heart. He asked her to breathe deeply, and cough, and follow his finger with her eyes. He asked her some questions and carefully recorded the answers on his clipboard. And then, he asked her to lie back on the examining table.

"Let's check out that hip," he said.

When Sarah had reclined, and her white cotton gown had been pulled discreetly away to one side, the doctor's look of casual good cheer turned to surprise.

"What happened here?" he asked, as he traced a large scar on Sarah's hip with one finger.

"That's from a bad burn I had, as a child," she explained. Sarah looked across the little room at Joan, who was regarding her with sudden, wary interest. "Isn't it lucky," she said, more to her granddaughter than to the doctor, "that I didn't have to go through life having a scar like this where people could see it?"

The doctor made some noise of agreement and continued his examination. Sarah wasn't listening to him. Her bright eyes were locked on Joan's, and she beckoned her to come closer to the table.

"Come see it, Joannie," she said.

Joan hesitated for a moment, then stepped closer to where her grandmother lay, and leaned over to see the scar that was twice as old as she.

The sight made her catch her breath.

There, on Sarah's hip, were two large patches of scarred tissue. The skin had been badly puckered and twisted, but the shapes of the two scars were unmistakable.

They formed a perfect pair of child-sized feet.

In Strange Fate *(Clark Publishing, 1963), Sarah Tyler wrote that witches like Miss Addie Welch learned their craft not from books, but from other witches before them. In turn, each witch was permitted to pass on her own knowledge and powers—but to only one select individual.*

If Miss Addie ever chose a successor, that person never became known. The reputable witch of Balsam Grove died in 1924, and no one ever stepped forward to take her place.

Mad Molly

It was April 1833—a fine spring day in St. Louis. Down at the riverfront, the burly men who sweated on the docks and the paddle wheelers were celebrating the warm quality of the day the same way that they celebrated all the events in their lives, and marked the days that were not eventful, too: they had taken refuge in the dark taverns and were filling themselves with drink.

On this particular day, in one of the louder, wilder places along the docks, a stranger wandered in. She was an old woman, a crone wrapped in a ragged shawl, clutching a frayed carpetbag to her side. Even in the dim light of the tavern, she was plainly ugly. The hag's face was misshapen and scarred, and her gray hair hung in filthy, matted clumps. Though it was clear that she was missing all but a few rotting, crooked teeth, the woman attempted to win a few of the patrons over with an ingratiating smile.

"Oh, please, gents," she simpered, "won't you buy an old lady a drink? I've just come all the way from New Orleans, and I'd love a little bit of gin, I would."

She moved from group to group, shuffling through the sawdust that covered the thick plank floor. The men refused her outright or rudely turned their backs. Not one was willing to spend his drinking money on the wretched old woman. Finally, the bartender grew tired of her begging and pulled a heavy wooden club from behind the bar.

"Out!" he demanded, as he brandished the club in the crone's ugly face. "I'll not have my customers bothered by a foul-smelling old hag!"

The drinkers turned to watch the confrontation and were amused when the old woman dropped the carpetbag and raised her arms in a dramatically threatening pose.

"It's the devil's eye for you!" she shrieked. A few men started to laugh but stopped when they saw the crone's body stiffen into a grotesque pose. The shawl slipped off one bony shoulder as she began to jerk convulsively.

"Get her out of here!" someone yelled from the back of the room. "She's having a fit!"

There were murmurs of agreement, but no one seemed eager to touch the spastic old woman or her filthy rags. So they kept watching until her body became still and her bulging, bloodshot eyes focused upon the wary bartender.

"*O Surmy, Delmusan, Atalsloym, Charusiboa...*" she began, and her voice was guttural and menacing. "*Melany, Liamintho...*" she continued to chant. The rowdy crowd had become quiet and still as every one of the patrons stared at the disturbing sight.

Finally, the hag's incantation came to an end. There was a moment of absolute silence, and then the old woman formed her lined, puckered mouth into an "O." She exhaled a long, raspy breath in the direction of the bartender.

The man began to grow very red in the face. Several of the gawking spectators assumed that his changing complexion was due to rage and expected to hear him unleash his fury upon the crone. But those who were standing closest to him—the patrons who were leaning against the long, scarred bar—noticed that the bartender was trembling. Within seconds, the ruddiness in his face and neck had progressed to a shade that was nearly purple, and his eyes bulged from their sockets. The wooden club slipped

from his fingers and clattered dully on the floor. His lips parted once, and a wet choking sound slipped past them. Then the bartender's eyes rolled back into his skull until only the whites of them could be seen beneath fluttering lids, and he crumpled to the floor.

Several of the patrons called him by name. The man did not answer and did not stir, so a number of fellows rushed behind the bar to his aid. Immediately, they recognized that there was nothing they could do.

"He's dead!" said one man, his voice fraught with shock and disbelief. A few others tried in vain to find a pulse or breath or sign of life and were forced to agree with the original grim diagnosis. The bartender was dead, a victim of "the devil's eye."

Everyone in the tavern turned to look at the old woman. She stood calmly, once again gripping her moth-eaten case. She wore a small, satisfied smile upon her lips. "'Tis a pity," she said, to no one in particular. "I only wanted a little sip of gin."

One of the men standing behind the bar turned to the row of bottles that lined a shelf on the mirrored wall there. He grabbed several and thrust them toward the grinning crone. "Take these," he spat, "and get out of here! We don't need more of your trouble, witch." The old woman opened her bag and stuffed in as many bottles as would fit. The rest she tucked under her arm as she turned to leave.

The hag slowly crossed the tavern, retracing the shuffling steps she had taken earlier. A low murmur of voices took up behind her.

"Witch!..." the crowd began to chant, accusingly. "Witch!..."

The voices grew louder and bolder. A gob of spittle landed on the dusty wooden planks just behind the old crone's feet. "Devil's daughter!" someone yelled, drawing the support of two dozen voices that agreed.

The din reached its peak when the old woman reached the door. It came to an abrupt halt when she turned to face the room. The hag had total silence and a completely attentive audience. It was her moment.

"M' name's Molly," she said, in her cackling old-woman voice, "and what I know, I learned from the most powerful voodoo queens of New Orleans. I serve the dark master, but I'm willing to do business with any one of you—for a price."

She cast one final leering glance around the room, then opened the door and disappeared into the blinding April sun.

Within days, the story of Molly's powerful evil eye had spread throughout St. Louis, and she began to profit handsomely from her notorious reputation. Business owners paid her for the favor of not casting her malignant eye upon their shops. People of all sorts began to seek her out to help them overcome their enemies. Lovers paid small fortunes to gain the affections of those whom they desired, and paid even more dearly to eliminate the romantic competition. Using her menacing eye, mysterious spells and *juju* dolls, she plied her trade in the darkest, most dangerous corners of the frontier city.

Molly spent a large portion of her earnings on the gin that she loved so much, and so, it was convenient for her to hold court at the back table of her favorite shadowy bar. Sometimes there would be as many as three or four people nervously waiting their turn as Molly struck a bargain with whoever was sitting with her. Occasionally, snippets of her advice could be overheard. Quickly, stories of her successes spread. Inevitably, Molly's reputation as a powerful witch grew.

"Take a lock of his hair, and burn it while you sprinkle this powder from above," she told one weeping woman. Weeks later, the woman's neighbors were whispering what a wonder it was that her cruel husband had stopped using his fists on her.

"Bury this charm beneath your front step with a piece of gold," she advised an eager young shopkeeper. Within a month, his once-floundering business appeared to be flourishing.

"Bring me something that belongs to your wife's lover," she croaked to a humiliated husband. "I'll make a doll from it. Very powerful." The man did as she asked and, soon, his rival was dead.

Spells were cast, and deals were made, and the devil's business was conducted daily in that bar as Molly sat hunched over the table with her gnarled hands wrapped around a tumbler of liquor. Although all of her customers feared her, most felt they received fair value for their investment. But every so often, there would be someone who felt cheated.

One evening, a young man came into the bar seeking Molly the Witch. He was directed to her table in the dark back corner. Molly gestured to the chair opposite her, and the man sat down to talk. It wasn't long, however, before the discussion grew heated. Molly stood up and tried to strike her threatening "devil's eye" pose, but the man pushed the table roughly against her, knocking her down.

"I'll curse you and you'll suffer!" she screeched, as he stormed out of the establishment. "I promise you'll suffer!"

It was never known whether Molly made good on her threat. The next morning, the police discovered the old hag's dead body in the filthy alley behind the bar. Her skull had been crushed with a blunt weapon, and her tangled, matted hair was soaked with blood. The blow to Molly's head had most certainly caused her death, but the murderer had apparently wanted to be very sure, for there was also a stake pounded through her heart. The final touch was a crudely fashioned wooden cross, which had been carefully placed upon the corpse.

It was never determined whether she had been killed by the irate client or someone else. Undoubtedly, the witch had as many enemies as she did paying customers. Only one thing was certain: nearly two years after arriving in St. Louis, Molly's profitable but twisted reign of dark power had come to an end. There were those who rejoiced, and those who wept, knowing that they were once again required to find their own solutions to life's difficult problems.

In his book Strange Women of the Occult *(Popular Library, 1968), Warren Smith suggests that Molly may have been no more than a convincing con woman who built a profitable reputation on a hapless bartender's timely heart attack. But whether she was a truly skilled witch or a manipulative confidence trickster matters little in the end. Either way, she was a powerful character and a colorful addition to the history of St. Louis.*

Mother Damnable

Keith finished his last forkful of lasagna and pushed his greasy plate off to the side. He didn't leave the table, but it wasn't out of respect for Bonnie, who was still eating. It was because the sports report was about to come on the little television that sat on the end of the kitchen counter, and Keith never missed the sports report. He leaned back in his chair, lit a cigarette, and drained the last swallow of beer from the long-neck bottle that sat in front of him. He waited until a commercial break before he spoke to his wife.

"That frozen lasagna's pretty good. What are you eating salad for?"

"Trying to lose a couple of pounds." Bonnie sat at the table with a book opened in front of her. Reading was her dinnertime distraction of choice.

Keith grunted and turned back to the television. When a carpet-cleaning advertisement splashed across the small screen, he turned back to Bonnie for another 30 seconds of what passed for conversation between them.

"Whatcha reading?" he asked. She held up the cover, with its impossibly long title, for Keith to see. He squinted and, as Bonnie silently predicted, got through only a few words before he gave up.

" 'A Short Account of the Old Indian Witch, Wampo...Wampo...' God almighty!" he complained. "Is the book as long as the title?"

"Not quite," Bonnie said, dryly. "And it's 'Wampohama.' " Then the commercial ended, and there was no more talk between them until after Keith had been satisfactorily updated on all the sports statistics.

It was rare for Keith to show an interest in anything that Bonnie did, let alone maintain one. That evening, however, when he turned off the television and rose from the table, he returned to the subject of the book.

"What the hell are you reading about witches for, anyway?" he said.

Bonnie looked at him, trying to determine whether his curiosity was the least bit genuine. After a moment's assessment, she decided to give him a real answer.

"It's historical," she explained. "Wampohama was an old Native woman who died 300 years ago. It's kind of interesting, because she lived right here, right where Winnipeg stands today. The white settlers called her 'Mother Damnable.' She made all sorts of predictions, so really," Bonnie shrugged casually, "she was more what you might call a seer, or a prophet, than a witch."

"I say potato, you say po-tah-to," Keith philosophized. "And *I* say it's all a load of bull."

Bonnie felt disgust that was directed at both Keith and herself. *What did I expect, telling that to him?* she chastised herself. Keith was not known for his open mind. She knew better than to argue with him on such points, though, so when she responded, she kept her voice mild.

"Come on, Keith. Don't you think it's possible to know things through—I don't know—a sixth sense? Don't you believe even a little bit in intuition?"

Keith jabbed his finger dramatically in the direction of his eyes. "I believe half of what I see," he said, "and none of what I hear." Looking satisfied at having made his point, he left the kitchen.

There was the familiar slow burn, the simmering anger

just beneath Bonnie's skin, and it was not due solely to Keith's quick dismissal of her ideas. *I know something about you,* she thought at him. *I haven't seen it, I haven't heard it, and I can't prove a thing, yet. But I know.* She could have said these things aloud, but she chose not to. Instead she returned to her reading and pushed the remainder of her salad aside. She no longer had an appetite.

An hour later, Bonnie was drying the last of the supper dishes when Keith walked into the kitchen. He dropped his canvas equipment bag by the back door with a *thud.*

"Are you playing hockey tonight?" Bonnie asked. She managed to keep her voice light and casual, but she held her breath as she waited for a reply.

"It's Wednesday, isn't it?" said Keith, which told her all she needed to know. "Of course I've got a game. Late ice time, too, so don't wait up."

Keith walked out of the kitchen without a backward glance. If he had taken a moment to look at Bonnie, he might have noticed that she was holding a plate in one hand and a dish towel in the other, but had stopped doing anything with either. She appeared to be momentarily frozen. Her body had become still because her mind was racing.

Keith was lying. Bonnie knew that; for the first time she knew it as a fact, because she had read in the weekly paper that the local rink was closed for a few days for maintenance. *Is he that lazy,* she thought, *that he wouldn't even bother to check? Or does he think that little of me, thinks I'd never figure it out?* Somehow, that was as insulting as the infidelity.

For some time, Bonnie had suspected that Keith was actually playing naked hockey every Wednesday night; she just didn't know who his teammate was. That particular missing piece of the puzzle was the reason Bonnie had let the affair carry on so long. She was sure that if she confronted Keith with the little bit she knew, he would deny everything and cover his tracks. After all, what did she have? A hunch, a suspicion, a bit of information from a source that would make him laugh, if he ever found out about it. And whenever they fought, Keith had a way of twisting Bonnie's words, making her sound foolish to her own ears, until she doubted what she had earlier been sure of. *I can't risk that this time,* she told herself. *I have to wait until I know.*

A name: that's what she needed. Things would change once she had a name, because that would be a bit of information so powerful that it wouldn't matter who had told it to her.

Twenty minutes later, reeking of aftershave lotion, Keith kissed Bonnie goodbye. She stood at the living room window and watched him back out of the drive, and lingered long enough to see the tail lights of his car disappear around the corner at the end of the street. Then she turned off the television and walked out of the room.

At the back of the highest shelf in the cluttered closet of the spare bedroom were a number of books that Bonnie never dared to read at the dinner table. She pulled one of them out, along with a bag filled with tapered black candles and chalk. The braided area rug that dominated the sparsely furnished room was tossed into one corner. Then, using the chalk, Bonnie carefully drew a circle on the worn hardwood floor. The candles were set at regular intervals

around the circle, and she fumbled with a packet of bent paper matches as she lit them, one by one.

Bonnie and Keith tended to use the small spare room as a dressing area, so they had hung two large mirrors on opposite walls, facing one another. Usually, the double reflection was used for nothing more dramatic than checking the back of a hairstyle or the evenness of a hem, but that evening, as Bonnie turned out the overhead light, the mirrors created the magical illusion that the room was filled with flickering candle flames. Bonnie smiled as she took in the effect. It pleased her, but it did not surprise her. She had created that particular ambience once before.

Bonnie was trembling with anticipation as she stepped carefully over the candles and entered the circle. She sat cross-legged in the center. Her palms began to tingle and the gooseflesh raised up on her arms even before she began to read the chant that was used to summon. There was energy in the room, Bonnie was certain of it, and certain that she would be successful one more time.

After several moments, she closed her eyes and began to call the name "Wampohama, Wampohama..." Then, "Mother Damnable—you know everything, and I need to know one thing more." The candles flickered all at once, their flames nearly sputtering out and then whooshing back to full bloom. Bonnie didn't see it. Her eyes remained shut; her body swayed slowly and rhythmically.

Then, suddenly, she stiffened. Bonnie stopped moving, and her eyes opened wide. She met her own gaze in the wall mirror and exhaled with a shudder. Like a cloud in the glass, subtly superimposed over her own pale features, was the deeply lined and dark face of an ancient Native woman. The image was unstable, nearly liquid at its outer edges, but there was more strength and substance than there had been the last time. More power.

Bonnie smiled. She was about to find out who was Keith's mistress. Then, she was going to do something about it.

And the next time Keith laughed at her choice of reading material, she thought she might just tell him an interesting story.

On her deathbed, the Huron seer named Wampohama dictated a series of prophecies that were published as a small book, nearly 200 years later. The title of the volume is A Short Account of the Old Indian Witch, Wampohama, better known to the early settlers as Mother Damnable, Together with her Extraordinary Prophecies, already partially ful-filled, concerning the Future Destinies of What are Now Winnipeg, Manitoba, and the Great North-West.

According to John Robert Colombo's book Mysterious Canada *(Doubleday Canada, 1988), there are those who have interpreted Wampohama's predictions and judged them accurate. For example, she claimed that "All the land west of this [Winnipeg] shall remain wild and unpeopled for 200 years. Then it shall give food to the eastern tribes of men." Around 1900, the western provinces began to produce wheat, which, indeed, was exported to the East. It would seem that "Mother Damnable" had a fairly clear vision of things to come.*

The Prophecy

It was a frigid February night in Montreal. Outside Antoinette and Carl Hartley's shabby little home, the wind howled and whipped the freshly fallen snow until the streets had been polished to ice. Inside the house, muted lamplight cast dancing shadows upon the cracked plaster walls, and a fire burned warmly in the hearth. These would have been great comforts against the vicious elements had anyone stopped to notice them, but those who were in the Hartleys' cozy rooms gave no thought to the storm outside. They were too thoroughly focused upon the storm within.

Mrs. Hartley screamed. Her husband, who sat at her bedside holding a tightly bundled baby, looked anxiously at the matronly woman who stood at the foot of the bed, attending to his wife.

"Madame Donat, should this not be over? The baby is here—what could be causing her such pain?" Carl Hartley's voice brimmed with concern. Childbirth could be dangerous; he knew that. For weeks, he had harbored vague fears about the well-being of the baby to come. He had prayed that it would be healthy and strong. But as he held his fat, red, squirming son in his arms, he worried that his concerns had been misdirected. He tried desperately to remember whether, in all of his devotions, he had made a mention for the safety of his normally sturdy wife.

The midwife was a practical sort and seemed unruffled by Mrs. Hartley's continued writhing and wailing. She maintained a veil of calm over her features as she examined the woman, probing her belly with thickset, experienced hands. Finally, she smiled. It was just a small expression but, to Carl Hartley, it looked like a beacon of hope. The woman wiped Mrs. Hartley's face with a damp cloth and spoke gently to her.

"My dear, you have to keep pushing," the midwife said. Then, turning to the bewildered and worried Carl, she added, "I think you are about to have a surprise."

Indeed, they were surprised.

Thirty minutes later, Mrs. Hartley had stopped screaming. She appeared pale and exhausted, but, above all, relieved. Nursing at her breasts were two perfect, contented infants. Carl Hartley sat beside her, his jaw slack and his eyes dull with shock. Madame Donat, the midwife, had taken a seat at the kitchen table on the other side of the room and was hunched over some writing task in front of the flickering oil lamp.

The scene remained thus for a long period of time: Madame Donat scribbling away, and the Hartleys staring at their new family with stunned wonder. Then, at some point, Mrs. Hartley spoke in a low voice to her husband.

"Carl, what is it she's doing there?"

Carl Hartley blinked, and pulled his gaze away from his new children. He looked at the midwife and shook his head.

"I don't know," he said to his wife. "She is writing—perhaps she has some instructions to leave us." Carl Hartley truly hoped that was the case. Over the course of the night, he had gone from having no children to being the father of two, and he needed someone to tell him what to do.

Mrs. Hartley, however, did not think it was anything so mundane. "She looks nearly fevered, Carl," she whispered.

It was true. Madame Donat was sitting on the edge of her chair, with her upper body sprawled across the greasy cloth that covered the table. Her breathing was heavy, and small muttering sounds issued from her as she scratched out her frantic composition.

Carl Hartley stood up and took one or two nervous steps across the room. Before he came close to the woman, however, she had finished. With a loud sigh, she straightened her posture and dropped the pen with which she had been writing. Madame Donat took a moment to stretch her back and massage the cramped muscles of her right hand, then stood up and turned to address the Hartleys.

"Keep that compress changed regularly," she instructed. "And nurse those little ones every two or three hours. Remember to eat; you need to build your strength. I'll look in on you tomorrow afternoon."

Madame Donat began to dress in her drab, heavy, winter garb as she issued her standard list of orders. When she had finished speaking and had wrapped the final protective woolen layer around herself, she paused to survey the room. After a moment, she nodded, seemingly satisfied that everything was in order, and exited into the freezing night without another word. The new parents stared dumbly after her for a few seconds, and then Mrs. Hartley spoke.

"See what it was she was writing, Carl."

Carl Hartley walked over to the table, where a familiar book lay open.

"She was writing in our Bible," he said to his wife. Carl picked the book up, carefully holding it open so as not to smudge the spots of still-wet ink, and carried it back to the bedside. Then, with growing astonishment, the Hartleys read the words the midwife had written there.

> I attest and bear my sign and seal herewith and duly record that on this 20th day in February, in the year of our Lord, 1896, I have delivered of Mrs. Antoinette Hartley and her husband, Mr. Carl Geo. Clayton Hartley, one fine baby boy and one fine baby girl. The son and the daughter are healthy and sound and do not bear any marks or deformity. The son is to be called Carl Gerald. The daughter is to be called Edith Anne. I predict that they shall live extraordinary lives for three score and eight years and that they shall be blessed with the higher powers of God until the hour of five upon the fifth day of the fifth month at which time one will call upon the other to withdraw from this earth. So be it that this birth record and document shall forever attest to what I, the undersigned hath writ here:
>
> Her Hand and Seal at Montreal, Quebec
> Madelaine Donat, Midwife

Mrs. Hartley was repulsed.

"What sort of fortune-telling witch did you bring here!" she cried to her husband.

Carl Hartley wrung his hands and stammered out a defense.

"You needed help," he said. "Madame Dion could not come in the storm, and Madame Donat could. And she did well, really," he pleaded. "Obviously she has her eccentricities, but she did nothing wrong."

Mrs. Hartley would not be mollified. She closed the Bible and pushed it into her husband's hands.

"We need a new Bible," she said, curtly. "We can ill-afford it, particularly with two new mouths to feed, but I'm not comfortable with this one that has been spoiled with evil predictions. Also, you will go looking for Madame Donat in the morning, and tell her that I require no more of her services."

The baby girl began to mewl, and Mrs. Hartley turned her attention there.

"Hush, Edith Anne, hush," she soothed. "Don't wake your brother, now."

Then Mrs. Hartley stopped still, as a disturbing thought occurred to her.

"Carl," she said. "Did you tell her what we had chosen for baby names?"

Carl Hartley thought carefully.

"No," he shook his head. "I was too distraught to mention it."

"That's odd, then," said Mrs. Hartley, who had grown a shade more ashen. "She might easily have guessed that we would name a son after you, but how did she know that we wanted to call our daughter Edith Anne?"

"Perhaps I did say something," said Carl Hartley, although he knew that he had not. Then, hoping to avoid further discussion of the matter, he took the Bible with the strange prophetic inscription and tucked it into the bottom of his clothing chest. There, he felt certain, his wife would never again be bothered by the sight of it.

He was right: Antoinette Hartley lived for another 42 years and never again laid eyes upon the Bible with its one page of spidery handwriting that predicted the lives and deaths of her children.

Carl Gerald and Edith Anne grew up together, but it was not until they began to live separate lives as adults that they became aware that they shared an uncanny ability. As Madame Donat had phrased it, they had been "blessed with the higher powers of God."

Edith Anne moved to Pennsylvania and married a wealthy coal merchant. Carl Gerald followed, for the sake of a job that had been promised him by his new brother-in-law. One day, as Carl Gerald worked in the coal yards, a sudden fire broke out. The small crew began to battle the blaze, but the situation looked grim, as there was no way to summon help: the first thing the fire had destroyed was the telephone line leading into the yard.

Fortunately, it seemed that a phone call was unnecessary. Sixteen miles away, Edith Anne somehow knew that something was wrong.

"There's a fire," she told her husband. "Carl Gerald and the other men are fighting it right this minute, and they need help!"

Edith Anne was so insistent, her husband tried to phone Carl Gerald at work. When his call would not go through, he gathered a group of volunteer firefighters and drove to the coal yards. They arrived in time to stop the blaze before it created any serious damage. Disaster had been averted, and Carl Gerald and Edith Anne realized that they were able to communicate telepathically.

The unique ability seemed to present itself in times of high emotion or stress. In 1938, Carl Gerald returned to

Canada for a visit and found their mother to be in frail health. The elderly woman refused to let anyone call Edith Anne, saying that it would be foolish to cause her worry. Within days, however, Edith Anne arrived with a suitcase. She said that the minute Carl Gerald had seen their mother, she—several hundred miles away—had known that something was wrong. Indeed, something was wrong, and five days after Edith Anne's arrival, Antoinette Hartley passed away.

When Carl Gerald retired, in 1958, he was still a bachelor. With time and a bit of money on his hands, he decided to take a tour of the United States. While he was gone, Edith Anne was struck by a sudden, incredible flash of knowledge.

"Carl Gerald has married!" she told her family and friends. "After all these years, can you believe it?" The people who knew Edith Anne well believed it without a doubt. They were accustomed to accuracy regarding the psychic messages she received about her brother. When Carl Gerald finally sent a letter from California to announce the news, no one was surprised, least of all Edith Anne.

In June of 1963, Edith Anne received a clear vision of a decidedly less happy event in Carl Gerald's life. He and his wife were driving from Oakland to Pasadena when their vehicle left the road. At precisely the time that it happened, a vision of the crash played out like a terrifying movie in Edith Anne's head. The concerned woman didn't even bother to confirm the news. She packed a bag and flew to California, where she stayed until her brother and sister-in-law had recovered from their injuries and were once again well enough to care for themselves.

Edith Anne and Carl Gerald maintained their psychic connection for nearly one more year. Then, at 5 AM, Eastern

Standard Time, on May 5, 1964, the final portion of Madelaine Donat's prophecy was fulfilled.

Edith Anne's first waking thought was of potato salad. *I really must remember to use less mayonnaise,* she scolded herself, as she blamed the pain in her chest on indigestion. But, as the feeling intensified and she became more fully conscious, she realized that something more serious than the previous evening's picnic supper was causing her to suffer.

She threw back the light chenille bedcover and felt a bolt of paralyzing pain shoot up her left arm. Edith Anne moaned and clutched her right arm across the lace bodice of her nightgown. Weakly, she called her husband's name, but he was a sound sleeper. Edith Anne was not, which was why the couple slept in twin beds and why the one person who could help her was snoring soundly on the other side of the room.

A fresh wave of agony swelled and tightened like a vise in Edith Anne's chest. *Dear God, help me!* she screamed inside her head. Aloud, she was able only to whimper, as her throat had constricted cruelly and her lungs were gripped by invisible iron bands. Small drops of cold perspiration began to dot her forehead and trickle down her neck. She guessed that if she remained in her bed, sweating and gasping for air, she would have only minutes left. The next stone of pain that hit her would be fatal.

She swung her feet off the bed and used her right arm to push herself to a sitting position. With tremendous effort, she slid forward and stood. Edith Anne managed to take two staggering steps before she crashed to the floor.

She fell hard, clawing at the wall and the nightstand as she went. A small, framed picture was dragged downward, tearing away a ragged strip of peach-and-white-striped wallpaper. The nightstand tipped, and a water glass and a little ceramic jewelry box skidded across its surface before thudding dully on the thick beige carpet. The cord of the bedside lamp got wound around Edith Anne's flailing arm. She pulled it simultaneously out of the socket and off the table. The satiny pleated fabric shade, for which she had once spent an entire morning shopping, was crushed mercilessly between her body and the bed.

"Edith Anne?"

She could hear her husband's groggy voice, but it seemed distant. At that moment, Edith Anne was focused entirely on what was happening within her. Something was coming; she could sense it, like a rising tide, and she braced herself for another torturous blow.

It never came.

Instead, Edith Anne went limp. In an instant, the agony had left her body. It would have been a great relief, except that the dark space left in its wake was too vast. The vacating pain had taken something with it, some quietly humming presence that Edith Anne had known for all her life. She knew what it was, and she screamed.

"Carl Gerald is dead! Oh, my god, he's *dead!*"

"Edith Anne!" Her husband's voice was closer now. It cut through the darkness, and some detached portion of Edith Anne's mind sensed that he was beside her on the floor, only inches away.

"Let me turn on some light," he was saying. "This damn lamp is broken."

"No," Edith Anne sobbed, "it isn't. I've got the plug." She was still tangled in the cord of the lamp and was clutching the end of it against her trembling, sweat-soaked body. She pushed herself up to her hands and knees and began to crawl across the carpet.

"Oh, poor Carl Gerald," she moaned, over and over, as she groped the wall looking for the outlet. She found it and inserted the plug.

There were three brilliant flashes of electric-blue light. Edith Anne screamed. Her eyes bulged and her mouth twisted grotesquely. Small tendrils of smoke curled up from the metallic brush rollers she wore in her hair. Then there was silence, and darkness, and Edith Anne was dead. Her fingers, damp with perspiration, had touched the prongs of the lamp plug as she had pushed it into the electrical outlet.

It was the fifth hour of the fifth day of the fifth month, three score and eight years after the Hartley twins were born. Carl Gerald Hartley lay dead of a heart attack, in California, only moments before Edith Anne was electrocuted, in Pennsylvania. One had indeed called upon the other to "withdraw from this earth," and so, the midwife's strange prophecy had been fulfilled.

According to Robert Tralins's book ESP Forewarnings *(Popular Library, 1969), the family Bible that contained the midwife's inscription was found among Carl Gerald Hartley's possessions following his death. Along with the Bible were several journals documenting the strange events*

of the twins' lives, and a note stating that Edith Anne had never known of the prophecy.

In other times, midwives were often believed to be witches who wanted to be close to newborn babes so that they could either kill them or offer them to Satan. The belief likely stemmed from the fact that powerful women who possessed special skills—particularly those determining life and death—were both threatening and suspect. In this case, however, it would seem that the midwife, Madelaine Donat, certainly did exhibit knowledge or talent that went beyond the realm of ordinary folk medicine. It would be interesting to know, of all the families she must have attended to, how many later discovered a strange, prophetic inscription in their family Bible.

The Hex

Louisa and Hester had been friends for as long as anyone could remember. They were as different as the sun and the moon—Hester was a bustling, practical woman with a large family and a busy life, and Louisa was a meek and dowdy spinster—but they lived near one another on their little eastern Pennsylvania farms, and one fact of rural life was that proximity was a necessary basis of friendship.

There was little to do in Louisa's home. She had only herself and her brother, Emil, to cook and clean for, and he did all the farm work. Hester, by contrast, had a house full of children and grandchildren to look after, and her list of chores was always longer than her day. For this reason, it was always Louisa who visited Hester's home, weaving herself into the fabric of daily life there.

Hester had one married daughter named Anna, who lived a mile or so down the rutted dirt road that wound through the district. Anna had just had her first baby, a smiling boy named Frank. When he was nearly six months old, it was decided that little Frank would start spending his days with Hester, so that Anna could be of more help to her young farmer husband.

Hester was pleased, and told Louisa of the plan.

"Don't you have enough to do, already?" asked Louisa. She was sitting in Hester's kitchen, watching her friend hand out sweet buns and cups of milk to the assortment of grandchildren who were already in her care.

"Ah, but what's one more little bundle?" said Hester. "And he's so sweet, Louisa. Wait 'til you see him."

Louisa only shrugged. But the next day, she did see little Frank, and her indifference left her entirely.

"He's so bright!" she exclaimed. "And so handsome! I never knew, Hester—I've seen babies before, but I never knew that one could be so delightful!"

Hester only chuckled and went on with her baking. It had been nearly two hours since Louisa had wandered across the road for a visit. For that entire time, she had been settled into Hester's big maple rocking chair with her arms around the baby. She was full of compliments for little Frank: he had the rosiest cheeks, the pudgiest legs and was clearly more clever than any other child so young.

"I dare say you're smitten, Louisa," smiled Hester.

"I couldn't love him any more if he was my own,"

replied Louisa with an intensity that, for some reason, made Hester slightly uncomfortable.

The next morning, when Anna brought Frank to his grandmother's house, there were shadows under her eyes.

"I didn't sleep well," she told Hester. "I was up through the night with the baby." Anna explained that little Frank had slept soundly until the stroke of midnight, when he awoke with a scream.

"Then, for half an hour, he was twisting and turning as though he was in pain. And crying; he was crying so pitifully the whole time! Finally, at 12:30, he fell asleep. But it wasn't a proper, restful sleep, Momma. I was so worried, I watched over him most of the night."

Hester clucked her tongue sympathetically and settled little Frank into his pram.

"Poor angel," she soothed. Then she smiled at Anna. "It was just a bad night. All babies have them," she said, reassuringly. "Tonight, he'll likely sleep as though he's floating on a cloud."

But the fact was that he did not. For the next two mornings, Anna arrived looking pale and drawn, carrying her listless little boy. Each night had been the same. Baby Frank would begin to scream and thrash about at midnight, and would not stop until half past the hour. Then, he would fall into an exhausted sleep in which he rarely stirred and seemed barely to breathe. Anna was consumed with worry, and after three days and nights, Hester had become concerned, too.

"We'll get the doctor to take a look at him," she decided. "It's probably only wind, but let's be certain."

The doctor did look at little Frank, and could not say that he was suffering from excessive gas or any other ailment. He gave the women some drops for the baby, saying that they would help him to sleep. Frank was given the drops that evening and did sleep quite soundly—until midnight. Then the screaming and writhing began, and continued for the full 30 minutes, until poor Anna was in tears and tearing at her hair.

"It's a terrible thing, Louisa. I don't know what to do." The children were all playing outdoors, the breakfast dishes had been cleared, and Hester was spending a rare moment in comfort. She was sitting in a cushioned chair, with her large hands wrapped around a mug of tea.

Louisa had claimed her usual spot in the rocking chair and was holding baby Frank. The infant lay passively in her arms, his eyes dull and uninterested. The rosy cheeks that Louisa had lavished with praise only a week earlier had become waxen, but she did not seem to mind. If anything, Frank's malaise endeared him to Louisa even more.

"Poor, darling, sick thing," she cooed. Then, to Hester, she confided, "Some babies are not meant to thrive, you know. You're right, it *is* a terrible thing, but there's nothing to be done about it. You mind the other children, Hester, and take care of your chores. I don't mind sitting with the poor, sick baby. I'll come every day," she promised. And she did.

Baby Frank had his bad spells every night. Anna walked around in tears most days. And Hester, who was accustomed to identifying and solving problems in her pragmatic way, developed a constant furrow in the middle of her brow. Only Louisa—who scurried across the road faithfully each morning, wearing a ready-made look of concern—seemed to actually flourish under the circumstances.

One hot afternoon, Hester walked quietly out on the verandah in search of a cooling breeze. Louisa, who was cuddling baby Frank on the porch swing, didn't hear her friend coming. She was focusing too intently upon the child, uttering words to him that Hester was never meant to hear.

"You're mine; yes, you're mine, my precious boy. That you were born to the wench Anna is only an accident of nature. We have ties that are stronger than blood, don't we, little Frank? And I promise, I will visit you every night, until you can be with me always."

Louisa's normally bland features were twisted into an expression of spite. The words she said were less spoken than they were hissed and, instead of holding the baby, she seemed to be clutching greedily at him.

Hester was paralyzed with horror—but only for a moment. Then she marched over to her old friend and snatched her grandson away before Louisa was able to object. With her free hand, Hester then took a firm hold of Louisa's doughy upper arm and lifted her out of the swing. In a half dozen great strides, she dragged the startled old spinster across the worn wooden porch and down the steps that led to the front path. Then, with a shove that nearly sent Louisa sprawling on her knees, Hester sent her away.

"You're not welcome here," she declared. "Not until you've examined your conscience and made your peace with God. Now, *go!*" she shouted. Louisa, rubbing at her bruised arm and casting fearful glances back over her shoulder, hastened down the path and across the road towards her home.

Hester stood on the porch watching her go, feeling more energetic than she had in days. She patted little Frank on one ashen cheek.

"Don't worry, Frank," she said. "Our problem is half solved." Then she went back into the house and collected together all of her brooms and a number of crucifixes, preparing for the other half of the solution.

"Louisa is a hex."

Anna stood stock-still in the middle of her mother's kitchen and listened to the unbelievable words.

"Momma, you aren't serious," she finally said.

"I'm quite serious," said Hester. "It's Louisa who's been visiting Frank at night, causing him pain and sickness. She wants that baby, and she means to have him. I mean to stop her."

The older grandchildren were wide-eyed and intrigued. "Grandmomma, Grandmomma, what's a hex?" they chimed. They had witnessed the scene between Hester and Louisa and knew that something terribly interesting had to be happening.

Hester sat the children down in front of her, and addressed them in all seriousness. "A hex," she said, "is another word for an evil witch, one who takes her power from the devil. Now, there's no need to be afraid, as long as you do as I say." The children held their breath and waited for their grandmother's instructions.

"Whenever you see Louisa, I want you to cross your fingers, like this," Hester held up her own hand to demonstrate, "and then hold your hand behind your back. If she speaks to you, you say quietly, to yourself, 'In the Name of the Father, Son and Holy Ghost.' If you do this, you'll always be safe."

Hester made each of the children say "I promise, Grandmomma." Then she turned her attention to Anna.

"I'll tell you the same thing, daughter," she said. "Fear won't help you, and there's no need for it. It's knowledge and vigilance that will save little Frank. Now, do as I say..."

Hester brought out the brooms and told Anna that she was to place one upside down in the back of every door that led into her home. She was also to put one behind the door of the room in which little Frank slept.

"They can come down by day," she said, "but put them back at sundown. And be sure to bless each one daily, in the name of the Holy Trinity, while you make the sign of the cross over the broom head."

Anna nodded solemnly. "And what are the crosses for?" she asked.

"The crosses are to be blessed by a minister," said Hester. After a moment's thought, she added, "Don't be too specific; just say that you want your son protected from all evil. Then put one around his neck, one in his crib, and one in his carriage. Place them as close to his heart as possible."

"Is that all?" asked Anna.

"I have only one thing left to say," added Hester. "Don't let the hex catch you off guard. They can be fiendishly clever, Anna, and know that, given time, you will be lulled into thinking that the danger has passed."

Hester took Anna firmly by the shoulders and leaned in closely, so that their noses were very nearly touching.

"Follow these instructions faithfully, until he reaches the age of five," she said, "and, God willing, your son will live to be a man."

Anna went home with Frank, and the crucifixes, and all of her mother's brooms. She did everything that Hester had told her to do, despite her husband's scoffing. Then she lay awake, in the cot beside her small son's crib, and waited for midnight.

Anna was so weary that, despite her apprehension, she drifted off to sleep. She was startled to consciousness, just moments after the clock struck 12, by a terrible cry outside the bedroom door.

It was a sound of horror, but also of surprise, as though someone had been suddenly and unexpectedly frightened. Other sounds followed, but they were howls of pain—distinctly different from the first cry. The loud screams continued for a few minutes, then became low moans that retreated into the distance. Throughout it all, and for the first time in many nights, little Frank slept undisturbed in his crib.

At the very same time, a mile or so up the rutted dirt road, Louisa's brother Emil was wakened from his sound sleep. He could hear his sister, shrieking and cursing, and leaped out of bed to go to her aid.

"Louisa!" he cried out, as he threw open the bedroom door. Then, Emil was struck speechless by the strange and frightening thing that he saw.

The bedcovers lay in a heap on the floor. Louisa twisted and writhed in the bed, holding her arms protectively in front of her face. There was no visible force fighting her, but she flinched and recoiled as if being assailed by blows. On the cheesy white flesh of Louisa's legs and arms, where they peeked out from beneath her modest cotton night-dress, Emil was stunned to see a number of rising, angry, red welts.

"Louisa..." he muttered, weakly, but she did not answer. It was quite some time before the strange battle came to an end. When finally it did, Emil's sister lay panting, sweating and covered with bruises, in the middle of her own bed.

"Would you like some tea?" Emil asked timidly, because it was the only thing he could think of to say. Louisa, who could barely move, still managed to cast him a look so dark that he decided to return to his own bed and give his sister her privacy until the morning.

It was several weeks before Louisa dared to knock at Hester's door. When she did, she was appropriately meek and contrite, and armed with excuses.

"I haven't been well, Hester," she said. "I've been weak and bedridden for nearly a month, and before that—well, I think I wasn't myself for quite some time."

Hester gave her old friend the coldest of greetings but allowed her to enter the house. She made tea, and the two women settled into chairs at the kitchen table. A terrible, uncomfortable silence settled heavily between them. Eventually, though, Louisa was unable to contain her curiosity.

"Please tell me, Hester," she pleaded, "is the poor, darling baby well?"

Hester nodded stiffly, but said nothing. Louisa took a small sip of tea and plucked nervously at her clothing.

Then, summoning all her courage, she made one final request.

"May I see him?" she asked, then hastened to add, "I won't touch him, I promise you. I know...he's been ill."

There was a long and weighty silence as Hester considered Louisa's plea. Finally, she rose from her chair and motioned for Louisa to follow her outside.

"He's sleeping in the backyard," she said, "and we must be sure not to disturb him." Her voice communicated an unspoken but clear warning. Louisa nodded her agreement.

As soon as Louisa caught sight of the familiar pram, however, she forgot all her promises and resolutions.

"Sweet little Frank!" she squealed. "Let me see how you've grown!"

She impulsively reached for the baby, then recoiled, as though bitten. For the first time, Louisa noticed the crosses that hung around the child's neck and in his carriage. She drew her breath in sharply and stumbled several steps backward. Then, mumbling something about not yet being well enough to visit, she went home. Hester watched Louisa retreat and noticed that, despite her professed "illness," the woman was moving at twice her normal pace.

Louisa did visit occasionally thereafter. She never stayed long, though, and she kept her distance from little Frank, who eventually grew into a robust boy. If she did indulge her wicked impulses in any way, it was not around Hester, for Hester had shown her that when one possessed the proper information, it was not at all difficult to deal harshly with a hex.

The true tale upon which "The Hex" was based was originally written by E. Linder Nalesnyk for Exploring the Unknown *(October 1964, vol. 5, no. 2), and was later included in Susy Smith's book* Adventures in the Supernormal *(Pyramid Publications, 1968).*

In her introduction to the story, Smith mentions that many houses and barns in eastern Pennsylvania are decorated with "hex signs." The purpose was never decoration, however. Many of the German settlers in that area believed fully in the power of the signs to ward off evil spells.

Immigrants brought their superstitions to the new country, as surely as they brought their possessions. The ability of brooms to ward off witches was another age-old belief that traveled from Europe. Generally, however, the brooms were thought to be effective not as weapons, but as distractions. The theory was that the witch would become so obsessed with counting broom straws that she would be left with no time for evildoing.

Part Two

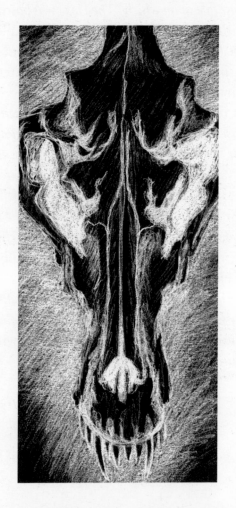

Werewolves

Hombre lobo. Loup garou. Lupo manaro. Lobo home. *Every Western European language has a name for the creature known in English as a "werewolf."*

That proves that the legends are widespread. The truth is, they are also enduring. Tales of these fierce, shape-shifting creatures date back to Greek and Roman times. The original "lycanthrope" was King Lycaeon of Greek mythology, who was turned into a wolf for displeasing Zeus.

While Zeus had his reasons for punishing Lycaeon (the king sacrificed a child, in an attempt to concili-ate the deity), folklore abounds with stories of those who become afflicted with the werewolf curse through no fault of their own. It has been said that children who are conceived during a full moon or born on Christmas Eve become werewolves, as do people who unwittingly drink from a watering hole frequented by wolves or eat the flesh of a lamb that has been slain by a wolf. Of course, those who sur-vive a werewolf attack are also doomed to become such a beast themselves—and it is this legend that has been employed most frequently by Hollywood moviemakers.

Werewolves are arguably the most fearsome and violent of all supernatural creatures—when they are in their wolf-like state. But most of the legends contend that these beasts maintain a human side as well, and during the periods when their human nature presides, they could be any of our friends or neighbors.

This dichotomy is a large part of what fascinates us about werewolves—for when the moon is full, there's no one we can trust...

The Pennsylvania Wolf Man

It was 1898. The wolves were bold that year in Northumberland County, and many conversations were held over supper tables about how the problem could best be handled. One particular evening, in one particular farmhouse, the Paul family discussed the situation over steaming bowls of stew.

"Albert Varney said that one of the beasts pulled a lamb out of his flock in broad daylight," said Daniel Paul, as his wife, Elizabeth, set a plate of bread in front of him. "They have no fear, no fear at all. It's only a matter of time before we lose animals as well."

"It's not the sheep I'm worried about, Daniel." Elizabeth cast a worried glance in the direction of the Pauls' 12-year-old daughter, May. May was their only child, and it was her job to tend the sheep. "I wish that May could be closer to the house, where I could keep my eye on her. After all, she's only a child. George could go out with the sheep, could he not?"

Daniel Paul shook his head gruffly as he bit into a thick slice of heavily buttered bread. "We've been over this," he said, around his mouthful of food. "May's able to watch the flock, but she'd be no help to me with some of the heavier chores that need doing around here. I need George with me."

George was a young farmhand, no more than 19 or 20, who had been with the Pauls for more than two years. He was quiet and hardworking and had proven himself trustworthy. Little by little, the small family had gathered George into their fold. He might have slept separately, in his tidy, comfortable loft in the barn, but he ate his meals with the Pauls, at their table, as one of them. He usually said little at mealtime, unless it was to report some bit of farm business to Daniel or to pay a clumsy compliment to Elizabeth about the food. This night was no different. George spooned up his stew and tore his bread, and if he had an opinion about what was being discussed, he did not offer it.

Across the heavy wooden table from George sat May Paul. Though the girl was several years his junior, she appeared more confident and was more outspoken than George in any given situation. Not that May was brash; quite the contrary—she was sweet and good and easy to love. It was just that because she had been well loved all her life, May was comfortable with her place in the world. She found it easy to speak her mind, particularly about things that affected her.

"I don't worry about the wolves, Mother. Neither should you," she said.

"Well, I *do* worry!" Elizabeth Paul shuddered. "When I think of what could happen..."

"Don't frighten the child, Elizabeth!" Daniel Paul cast a stern gaze at his wife. The set of his features softened when he turned to speak to his fair-haired daughter. "Of course, it's not just wolves we have to worry about, is it?" Though everyone at the table knew what Daniel was talking about, no one spoke a word. The topic was a sensitive one.

"Has he been around lately, May?" Daniel kept his voice mild, but his eyes were dark. He was asking his daughter about The Stranger, a man who lived on a small piece of land a few miles away from the Pauls' farm.

In the tight-knit Pennsylvania community where there were few outsiders and fewer secrets, The Stranger led a life so solitary, he was not even known by name. When he rode into town to make his occasional purchases, he never bothered to change his soiled work clothes or to comb his matted, gray hair. When the shopkeepers greeted him, he brushed them off with a surly glance. The Stranger had a miserable disposition, a jaundiced eye and a mysterious way. The good people who were his neighbors regarded him with suspicion and fear. They might have simply, and practically, dismissed him had he chosen to keep entirely to himself—but he did not. For The Stranger had an interest of some sort in young May Paul.

On most days, when May was tending her little flock of sheep, The Stranger could be found lurking in the shadows just beyond the open pasture. Sometimes, he watched her for only an hour or so. Sometimes, he would stay for most of the day, sitting comfortably on a fallen log that lay at the edge of the grassy clearing. He never spoke to the girl, never approached her, never acted inappropriately or threateningly. Still, when May told her parents about the visits in her casual fashion, Daniel and Elizabeth worried. For days, they mulled over what to do, eventually coming to the unsatisfying conclusion that there was little they *could* do. They warned May that she should never speak to The Stranger and that she should run back to the house if he approached her. Aside from that, the Pauls had their hands tied.

"Unfortunately, you can't persecute a man for being odd," Daniel told his wife, although it was clear that he wished he could.

"May! I asked you has he been around lately?"

May looked calmly at her father and nodded. "Nearly every day," she said, matter-of-factly. "He just sits and watches me, Father. It's really rather nice to have the company, even though we don't speak."

"Well." Daniel pushed his empty bowl away, leaned back and crossed his arms. "Well," he said again, maintaining his thoughtful pose. After a few silent moments, he seemed to arrive at a decision. He stood up, and the wooden legs of his chair scraped loudly against the rough plank floor.

"I'll tell you what we can do," he said. "I can't have George off lazing in the pasture all day long, but I can spare him for a short time here and there." Daniel turned to address his young helper. "Starting tomorrow, George, you can look in on May two or three times during the day and make sure all is well." Daniel glanced briefly at Elizabeth and added, "So her mother won't worry about the wolves..."

The next day was fine and clear, with a deep blue sky that stretched from horizon to horizon. George was repairing the roof of the hen house, enjoying the warmth of the sun on his shoulders, when Daniel Paul reminded him of his new duty.

"Take a break, George," the older man instructed. "I'll pound these last few nails while you walk out to the pasture to check on May and the sheep."

Obediently, George dropped his hammer and set off along the path that served as a shortcut to the grassy place where May spent her day with the flock. The route took him through the dense and shady woods. It was cooler there by several degrees, and George was enjoying the refreshment of it as well as the way the light fell through the leaf canopy in pretty patterns. When he reached the place at the opposite edge of the woods where the smooth dirt path widened and opened into the green pasture, he stopped. He told himself that a few more minutes of cool comfort might be nice. Though he was usually in no way a sneaky fellow, George reasoned that it would be best if May did not see him taking a little rest in the midst of the workday. To ensure that she did not, he ducked behind the thick trunk of an old oak, where he held a fine view of the open space while remaining secreted in the shadows.

The sheep were milling about like woolly clouds on a green grass sky. Watching over them, looking as golden as the sunshine, was May. The girl, caring for her flock, walking through the field with her faded print skirt swirling in slow motion around her, created a lovely pastoral scene. George watched May contentedly for several minutes, unmindful of the time that was passing. He might have watched for several minutes more had a dark movement on the opposite side of the pasture not broken his gaze.

It was a wolf, a powerfully built dark gray beast creeping alongside the pasture, just behind the outer edge of the woods. George knew that the animal would wait until it was within pouncing distance of a fat ewe before breaking out into the open. One particular sheep, oblivious to the danger, began to wander closer to the woods. George's heart leaped to his throat when he saw May jump up from the flat rock where she had been taking a moment's rest to run after the stray. He saw the wolf's eyes glinting from within the shadows of its hiding place. He saw May's bare feet running lightly across the grassy ground. He saw the wolf turn its

head ever so slightly and draw back its black lips as it turned its attention from the sheep to the approaching girl. And then he saw something he didn't understand.

The wolf was poised to leap out into the open when suddenly it recoiled, as if stung by some unseen missile. The animal let out a sharp, high yelp and nearly fell over its own paws as it scrambled backward, forgetting its intended prey. The wolf scurried for the cover of the thick underbrush, risking only one backward glance. Whatever the animal saw caused its tail to creep beneath its crouching body. The wolf slunk away, out of sight.

The animal's cry had caught May's attention. As George watched the last patch of gray fur disappear into the shadows and foliage, the girl was watching as well. Then she turned, seeming to sense that she had an audience. Her eyes found the young farmhand, who had, during the tense moments, moved several steps closer to the clearing. She smiled at him, and though the smile was nothing but sweet, George felt his ears burn, and he quickly looked away.

He had checked on young May; he had seen that she was fine. George could report back to Daniel Paul and return to the less confusing matter of the hen house roof. The young man turned away from the little shepherdess, planning to retreat, as had the wolf, to the shade and concealment of the forest path. As he turned around, however, George stopped cold. For there was The Stranger, sitting on the fallen log, watching over May and her flock.

George had not seen the man initially, as his wooden perch was on the same side of the pasture as the mouth of the forest path. He might have wondered how long The Stranger had been there, or whether he had caught George spying, but all normal thoughts had vacated his mind. As he looked at The Stranger, George was utterly spellbound by what he saw.

The man's face was shrinking.

That was George's initial impression, although he soon noted that the features were not shrinking so much as they were altering, changing shape. The changes were slight and the transformation smooth, but in the bright noonday sun, George was certain of what he saw.

The lower half of The Stranger's face—his nose, mouth and chin—appeared to be drawing back, toward his ears. The ears themselves were sliding down the man's skull and melting from an unnatural, elongated shape into their usual, round form. There was the hair, as well. As he first looked at the man, George thought that his face was overcast by a shadow. As the changes took place, however, it became obvious that there was a shade of coarse, dark hair that came low on The Stranger's brow and high on his cheekbones. As the very structure of the man's face melted into its familiar shape, the hair receded, crawling back into its follicles.

George gaped at the sight. At some point, he became aware of his stupidly hanging jaw and made a conscious effort to pull it back into place. He swallowed and felt a dry, uncomfortable clicking in the back of his throat. *Go*, he told himself. *Go now!* But before he could force his wooden legs to walk, The Stranger turned. With intense, glittering eyes, he looked at George.

He smiled.

And in the most horrible moment of all, George saw that the teeth bared in that expression were just a fraction of an inch longer than they should have been. But it was only for a moment, and then the effect was gone. The yellowed teeth shrank into the gums, became a little less uneven, a trifle more flat and dull. And then, it was over. A common fly droned past George's nose, signaling the return of normalcy.

George realized that he had been holding his breath. He let it out in a shudder, gasped in fresh air, and turned, searching the pasture for May. She was sitting on the large rock again, sunning herself, looking unshaken. George looked back at The Stranger. He appeared equally unruffled, perched serenely upon his log, casting his adoring looks at the girl. All looked well. George decided that before that changed, he would leave. He rediscovered the strength in his legs and ran all the way back to the farmyard.

"Took you a while," grunted Daniel Paul, who was clearly irritated at having to work so hard by himself on such a hot day. "Everything alright?"

George paused for less than a second before picking up his hammer. "May is fine," he said, and hoped that Daniel would not ask him to make another trip to the pasture that afternoon.

That night, as he lay wrapped in Elizabeth Paul's handstitched quilts in the cozy loft of the barn, George found it difficult to sleep. When finally he did doze off, he dreamed of dead lambs, their white wool matted with blood and their throats torn open by powerful, razor-sharp fangs.

Days passed. Then weeks and, eventually, months. The strange, frightening experience of that one hot afternoon slipped into distant memory for George and took on the dreamy quality of something half imagined. By the following summer, he had convinced himself that his head had been too long in the sun that day. Only occasionally, when George found May looking across the broad wooden supper table with a certain *knowing*, did he ever doubt his reasonable explanation.

George was not the only one whose fears became distant and dull as that time passed. When a full year had come and gone and none of the Pauls' sheep had been lost to the marauding wolf packs, Daniel was lulled into accepting that for some reason unknown to him, his flock was safe from attack. He decided to simply be grateful and let it lie. He and Elizabeth had also come to feel, not exactly comfortable, but *accustomed* to the eccentric attachment that The Stranger seemed to have to their daughter. The man seemed content to merely watch the girl and, while it was decidedly peculiar, the Pauls had ceased to think that his behavior was a real cause for concern.

The Pauls' friends and neighbors had not been so effectively calmed by the passing months, however. They continued to regard The Stranger with distaste and distrust, and continued to lose sheep to the fierce and fearless wolves. To deal with their feelings about the unpleasant outsider in their midst, the people of the community chose to shun him. And, attempting to deal with the problem of the wolves, they placed a $25 bounty on the head of each beast.

A neighbor of the Pauls, an old farmer named Thomas Worley, kept this bounty in mind wherever he went. He carried his rifle, slung over one bony shoulder, any time he ventured further than his own front yard, and always kept a keen eye searching for the profitable prey. He had experienced some success: one $25 reward had already been squirreled away in a sealing jar under the bed. If he could add the price of another wolf's head to it, Worley would be well on his way to the price of a fine new wagon to replace the rickety, rotting bucket that he drove. And so he carried his gun, and he spent long hours dreaming of how it would feel to put his hands on that money.

One morning, he showed up at the Pauls' farm, flushed with excitement. "Daniel!" he croaked, in his unsteady old man's voice. "Daniel, I need a bit of neighborly help from you, if you don't mind!"

Daniel Paul, who had been trying to right a toppled fence post, sighed before turning to face Worley. The elderly man was alone, caring for his few animals and little piece of land. He often needed a hand. Daniel Paul was a good fellow who was usually glad to help, but he was in the midst of a particularly busy day and did not want to stop. Still, he was polite.

"What is it you need, Thomas?"

"Help with a carcass." The old fellow beamed as he made the announcement. Everyone who knew Thomas Worley knew of his obsession with the wolves and the bounty money. There was no doubt what kind of carcass he was talking about.

"Got yourself a beast, did you Thomas? Good work."

The old farmer's chest puffed out with pride. "I did indeed. Just have to find it and bring it in now."

"Find it?" Daniel raised his eyebrows.

"Yep. Find it. You see, I was on my way home from Ben Scully's place last night, takin' the route that runs east along my place. I had my rifle with me—always prepared, you know—and I saw this rangy old wolf creeping across the road. Well, what with last night bein' clear, and with the full moon, I could see sharp as day. Took a shot at 'im, I did, and I hit the beast. Should've heard 'im howl! But he took off into the woods anyway. I knew I couldn't track 'im at night, no matter how much blood there was, but now, in the daylight, it'll be an easy bit of business. There's a good trail to follow. It's just the carryin' part that's hard on these old bones." Worley smiled crookedly and shook his thin arms for emphasis.

"Thomas, I'd like to help you, but today is difficult," Daniel said. "I have to mend this fence, or it'll be my own livestock you'll be shooting at, up on the road." The old man's face crumpled in disappointment, and Daniel Paul softened. "Of course, I guess that I could keep working here while George went with you."

"That'd be fine!" Thomas Worley beamed. "Real generous!" He turned to George, and added, "There might even be a dollar in it for you, young fella." He seemed to hear his own stinginess, and after a short pause, added, "or two."

"Go on then, George." Daniel gestured to his young helper. "But be smart about it. I expect you back in time to clean the barn." George nodded, and trailed off after the old man, who turned every few steps to wave his thanks to Daniel Paul.

One mile up the road, Thomas Worley pointed to a bit of trampled, scarlet-stained brush.

"That's right. Wolfie went in there, half dragged himself through the ditch, you can see. I hit 'im square on, I can tell you that. My guess is we won't have to go more than a dozen paces in before we find the critter."

As it turned out, the old farmer's guess was wrong. The wounded wolf had been strong, and Thomas Worley and George spent more than 10 minutes following the splatters of gore it had left as it dragged its wounded body through the forest. At the end of it, there was a disappointing moment when they thought they had lost the trail.

"Shoot," Worley said, in a depressed voice. "I can't see no more, George. Can you see where that wolf went to?"

George used one dusty hand to wipe the sweat from his forehead and left gray streaks there. It was hot even in the shade, and a dollar *(or two)* hardly seemed worth the trouble of tramping through the thistles and bushes looking for a dead wolf, let alone hauling the same dead wolf back to the road and then another half mile to Worley's yard. George was hot and tired and ready to suggest that the wolf had clearly gotten away with no more than a flesh wound when something caught his attention. In the deep green and brown shade of the woods, an unnatural patch of pale color glimpsed out from beneath a low, leafy branch. George stared at it for a moment, then walked over and pulled the foliage aside. It was a dead body. It was not a wolf's dead body.

"Lordy!" Thomas Worley was standing a good 10 feet behind George and making no attempt to move any closer. For the first time that morning, he wasn't thinking about the bounty money. It had become obvious that there would not be any bounty money. The county paid out $25 for killing a wolf, but reacted less favorably toward the killing of a man.

It definitely was the cold corpse of a man that lay, naked and bloody, on the forest floor. He had fallen on his side, with his knees pulled protectively up toward his belly and his fists clutched against his chest. Dried crimson streaks decorated his lean, white body. His clenched hands and forearms looked as though they had been dipped in paint. Beneath the man's chest, there was a sticky black circle where his blood had saturated the mossy earth.

George knew where the wound would be but had to turn the body to see the proof of it. The debris of leaves and twigs gave a scratchy whisper as George rolled the dead man to his back.

"The bullet hit his heart," he said to Worley. The old man looked relieved.

"Then it wasn't mine!" he nearly crowed. "There ain't no man could crawl this far off the road with a bullet in the *heart!* Thank the lord!" Worley sagged against the nearest tree, weak with relief. "For a minute there, I thought I done a terrible thing," he said. "My eyes ain't what they used to be, and moonlight or not, I thought I maybe mistook this fella..." he trailed off, and pulled a stained old handkerchief out of the pocket of his overalls. Worley wiped at his face for a moment, then turned back to George, who was crouched over the body.

"Whatcha doin' there?" he asked.

"Just looking." George was holding one of the dead man's clenched hands gently in his own hands. He pried the bloody arm away from the body and managed to open the fist just enough to see the fingernails that had cut their half-moon prints into the man's palms. They were ragged and caked with dirt and blood. They were long, too, longer than a man's fingernails usually were. In fact, the fingers them-selves were longer than normal, extending about an extra half inch between the first and second gnarly knuckles. George carefully placed the man's hand back on his chest and wiped his own fingers against the leg of his trousers with a vague sort of revulsion. His gaze moved up to the neck and face, where it looked as though the dead man had been beginning to grow a coarse, dark beard. There was a shade of hair on his ears, too. Ears that seemed to be placed just a little far back on the skull.

Worley still would not come any nearer to the corpse but seemed to be growing impatient with George's quiet investigation. The old man shifted his weight from one foot to the other, waiting for his young companion to offer a bit more information. Suddenly, he stopped fidgeting. His grizzled face fell, as a terrible possibility occurred to him.

"George! That ain't nobody we know, is it?"

George was using his thumb to push the dead man's upper lip away from his teeth. The teeth, he could see, were stained and broken. Also, just a fraction of an inch longer than they should have been. George recoiled and, again, wiped his hand roughly against his clothing. He stood and turned to answer Worley.

"No, Mister Worley," he said. "That's a Stranger."

In the end, they decided it would be best to bury the body where it lay. It was George's suggestion, and Thomas Worley, who was comfortable with his rationalization and didn't want anyone looking too closely at whether or not the bullet that killed the man came from his gun, readily agreed. The old farmer went back to his own house to fetch a shovel, and George did the rest. Worley recited a few scrambled passages from a sermon he had once attended, saying it seemed like the proper thing to do, even though he "clearly didn't have a thing to do with the fella's passing." Throughout it all, though, Thomas Worley couldn't bring himself to even once look at the dead man's face.

George had not returned to his own duties until very late afternoon that day. By that time, the fence had been completely mended, the barn cleaned, and Daniel Paul—who did it all on his own—was nearly too angry to speak. George had mumbled an apology, but it was barely acknowledged by his furious employer. It was just as well. An apology that had been accepted might have opened the door to an explanation, and George had no idea what he would have said. When he considered that, he was content enough to simply endure a few days of Daniel's silent wrath.

In the week that followed, George handled his chores with an extra measure of care, in an effort to smooth things over. One afternoon, when he had finished all the jobs that Daniel Paul had assigned him for the day, he decided that it was time to take care of one necessary bit of business of his own.

As George left the forest path and walked into the sunny green pasture, he could see May sitting on the rock that was her usual perch. She had her hair tied back in a thick braid, which accentuated the increasingly mature angles of her face. Although they had eaten bowls of sugary oatmeal together that very morning, it was somehow easier to *notice* May when she was out in this place where she spent so much time alone. What George noticed that afternoon was that May didn't look like a child anymore.

George made a bit of deliberate noise as he walked across the grass. May heard and turned to face him. She smiled her sunny smile and waved a greeting. George raised his hand in return.

"I didn't know Father still wanted you checking on me," she said. For a moment George wondered if May was teasing him. He detected nothing in the tone of her voice, however, and lowered his defenses a little.

"Your father doesn't know I'm here," he said, and in the pause that followed, he felt that it was May's turn to try to read between the lines. It was unusual to catch the girl the least bit off balance, and George found that he took no particular pleasure in it. He decided that it would be best to be direct.

"I've been thinking, May. About the wolves, that is. They're still around, and I was wondering if you might be a bit more concerned about them, lately."

May didn't ask why. She didn't say anything, and after a moment, George continued.

"I know a fellow who has some dogs for sale. Would you feel better out here with a fierce dog by your side, do you think?"

May smiled again, and there was a tinge of sadness to the expression.

"Thank you George. But there's no need."

George felt a flutter of panic in his stomach. Did she not know? He had always felt that certain things were easier to bear when nothing was acknowledged aloud. Suddenly, he feared that he would be forced to actually tell her about the day that he had been trying so hard to put out of his own memory. The anxiety gripped him only temporarily, however. As soon as May spoke again, he realized that she knew everything. Or, at least, she knew what was necessary.

"I did worry a bit, for a day or two. I thought I saw one of the big wolves watching me, waiting to see if I was truly alone. And I thought I was. But then he came back."

"Back?" George had intended to sound calm, but the word came out like a gunshot.

"Yes, back. In a way. I still see him, at the same time. In the same place..." May's voice trailed off and she turned slowly in the direction of the fallen log that had served as a seat for The Stranger who had been her dedicated admirer.

Her gaze lingered so long in that seemingly vacant spot, George could not resist asking her the question.

"Is he there now?"

May turned to look at George. She did not answer, but smiled.

"Don't worry about the wolves," she said, and he knew that he had been dismissed.

George worked for the Pauls for only a few months more. He found that he was no longer comfortable in his familiar surroundings. Eventually, with true regret, he told Daniel Paul that he would be leaving.

"Going where?" was Daniel's only question.

The man looked so genuinely devastated, George knew that it would be cruel to tell him the truth, to say, "Anywhere but here." So, instead, George said "Virginia" and pretended that he had an opportunity awaiting him there.

In the end, George did travel south—walking mostly and working for food and lodging along the way. He kept going until he felt that the distance was sufficient, and then he stopped. He found himself in North Carolina and stayed there for the rest of his days.

Occasionally, he thought about May Paul and her kind parents and the strange experience that they had shared. The years tended to put things out of focus, though, and George discovered that he eventually came to doubt his memories. It pleased him; it made everything simpler to live with. And it was a state more easily maintained when May's knowing glances were not being cast at him across the evening meal.

Many years later—George had a family of his own and was the age Daniel Paul had been when he had worked for him—George met a fellow whom he had known in those days. The man still lived in Northumberland County and still knew the Pauls. He told George that they were well, though Daniel was getting on in years and finding it more difficult to manage the work of the farm.

And May?

May was also well, the man reported. Never married. Still fine looking though, and still tending those sheep. The fellow chuckled a bit, but the smile faded quickly from his face.

"You know, people talk, sometimes," he said. "They say…Well, it's odd, isn't it?"

"What?" asked George, although despite the years and their softening effect upon the details of his memory, he was certain that he knew what his old friend was about to say.

"You know the problem with the wolves," the man explained. "It never quite goes away. Everyone loses an animal here or there. But May Paul…" the fellow shook his head in disbelief, then told George what he already knew. May Paul had been herding sheep for 25 years and never lost a single lamb.

For a few nights thereafter, when George laid his head on the pillow and closed his eyes, he was chilled by the images that played out in his mind. Images of a huge gray wolf with yellow teeth and glittering, intelligent eyes. Images of a man with those same intense eyes and a skull capable of shifting into a shape that was flat and broad and dark with bristly hair. Images of a lupine phantom watching over the object of his desire and affection for more than two decades.

As was his way, George didn't tell anyone. Eventually, he knew, the dark pictures in his mind would grow distant and would, once more, allow him to sleep.

This story stands out as one of the few lycanthropy cases on record where the human part of the beast was able to control his animal alter ego—to the extent of actually being protective of someone who was obviously a potential victim. That fascinating twist may have been the reason that the tale managed to survive through the generations. According to Bernhardt J. Hurwood (Vampires, Werewolves, and Ghouls, Ace Books, 1968), *as late as the 1960s, there were those in Northumberland County, Pennsylvania, who could tell you where The Stranger was buried. Among the locals, the site was known, simply, as "the wolf man's grave."*

Loup Garou

Jean Bertrand was sitting in his own comfortable chair, but awkwardly, as at that moment he felt like a visitor in his own home. He found himself rearranging his hands often, trying to look casual and failing. Fat William Porter, on the other hand, was leaning back easily, warming his feet by the wood stove, and looking for all the world like he owned the place. Of course, if all went well, he was about to.

The Englishman clucked his tongue and tapped his thick fingers against the piece of paper Bertrand had given him to read. It was a list, a carefully itemized account of Jean Bertrand's personal property. It began with the ornate trunk that his great-grandmother had traveled with as she sailed up the St. Lawrence River, prepared for a new life in a land that was then called New France. It ended with the sturdy dappled mare that Bertrand had purchased only one year earlier as he had watched his home come under British rule. Times were changing; the fact was even more painfully obvious to a man when he found himself having to sell off his past.

Porter sniffed loudly and tossed the list aside. He looked over at Bertrand with a condescending and humorless little smile.

"I'm sure you had a figure in mind," he said.

"*Oui*, of course," Bertrand stammered. "It is fair, I think, given the number of quality items..."

"How much?"

"Well, this would include everything on the list, even the pieces of jewelry..."

"I am busy, Bertrand. How much?"

Jean Bertrand told him. Porter emitted a mean, wheez-
ing burst of laughter.

"You've mistaken me for a charity," he said, and grunted
as he stood up. "Also, you have wasted my time. Now, if
you'll excuse me, I have real business to attend to." Porter
nodded curtly and turned toward the door. Bertrand tried
to not speak too quickly, but there was panic gripping his
chest and the desperate words spilled out.

"What, then? What do you think…? That is, what
would you give me?"

William Porter stopped with his hand on the door
handle. Though Porter had his large back to the room,
Bertrand could sense the smug smile upon his lips. When
he turned around, however, his face was bland and he
shrugged as though he had become uninterested in the
whole negotiation.

"I'll give you half," he said, bluntly.

Half. The previous moment's panic gave way to crush-
ing disappointment. *How far can I possibly go on half?*
thought Bertrand. He feared not far enough.

"But the furnishings alone," he protested, "they must
be worth that much! And the tack that hangs in the stable
is very nearly new!"

"Certainly," Porter nodded agreeably. "Everything you
say is true. And if you went to every door in Kamouraska
and sold the items one by one, you would likely fetch your
price. But you are in a hurry, I think, Mr. Bertrand." William
Porter paused to fix his narrowing gaze on Jean Bertrand.
"You are in a hurry and you wish to divest yourself of everything at once. Now, I can help you, but you must leave room
for me to take my profit."

Bertrand felt helpless. Everything the Englishman had said was true; he did not have the luxury of time or the advantage of indifference. He could sell to Porter, or he could abandon most of what he owned. Those were Bertrand's choices, so he did the only thing he could do.

"Half, then," Bertrand said, and nodded. He could barely stand to look at the expression of delight that spread across William Porter's face.

"Splendid! A wise decision!" he boomed, and eased his bulk back down on the wooden chair. With one hand, he gestured to a bottle that Bertrand had on a high shelf, above the wash basin. "Let's toast to having struck a deal, shall we? A drink serves as well as a handshake and a signature, that's what I always say."

Then perhaps you should pull your own flask out of your pocket, Bertrand thought sourly. He said nothing, though, and obediently brought down the bottle and two mugs. He pushed aside the clutter that was on the table—the bit of lunch, for which he had had no appetite, and an issue of the *Quebec Gazette*—and set one mug in front of his beaming visitor and one at his own place. He poured a measure of amber liquid into each. Porter raised his drink and offered an enthusiastic toast.

"To our agreement, then!" Without waiting for a response from his host, Porter gulped down a mouthful of the liquor. It brought on a coughing fit that reddened his doughy face. When he was finished, he eyed his drink suspiciously.

"Not exactly the best, is it?" he said.

Bertrand ignored the insult and sipped from his own cup. He reasoned that he would only have to be polite for as long as it took Porter to swill his drink and enjoy a brief bit of gloating. Then he would be left, blessedly alone, to nurse his stinging misery and entertain his poisonously uncharitable thoughts.

Porter was oblivious to how unwelcome he was. Once again, he was comfortably reclined in his chair, looking around the room with interest.

"That painting, there," he pointed to a muted water-color landscape that graced one wall, "that should bring a good price."

"It has great value," said Bertrand. After a pause, he added, "It was my mother's."

Porter grunted. "Your sentiments won't be worth anything extra to my buyer," he said. "But, still."

The two men sat in silence for a few moments. Bertrand imagined that Porter was surveying the room and running calculations in his head, and so was surprised when he looked up from his mug and found that the Englishman was slyly surveying him. When their eyes met, Porter offered a knowing little smile.

"You're not much of a negotiator, are you?" he said.

Bertrand felt too weary to rise to his own defense and merely shrugged.

"No. You're not," Porter answered his own question. "But I suppose you just want to go. Looking for greener pastures, I think. It's never gone too well for you here, I know that much."

Bertrand felt exposed and humiliated. "I've done well enough," he retorted. "My reasons for going are personal." He glared at Porter with what he hoped was enough rancor to put a stop to the personal comments, but not so much that it would spoil the deal that had just been made. It was a balance that required great effort. Porter did not seem put off so much as he seemed amused.

"Mmm," he said. "Is that so." His eyes narrowed a little when he added, "Are you quite sure you're well enough to travel, though, Bertrand? It would appear that you've been in a scuffle."

Bertrand's right hand flew to his neck, to cover the fresh, white bandage that he wore there. He had been careful that morning to put on a shirt with a high collar, but it had failed to completely conceal the dressing. He imagined that William Porter, with his cunning businessman's eyes, had noticed it the minute he had walked in the door. Bertrand wondered if he had further surmised, from the stiffness of his movements, that there were bigger bandages covering deeper wounds, winding across his rib cage from front to back.

"It is nothing. A little accident," was all he said.

"What kind of accident?"

Bertrand did not answer, and the stubborn set of his jaw indicated that he did not intend to. He needed Porter's money, it was true, but Porter also stood to make a tidy profit from their business dealing. He did not owe the Englishman anything further.

William Porter seemed annoyed when he did not receive an answer to his direct question. He pretended to make fun of the situation, but his eyes had grown dark.

"A secret, eh? I wonder if I can guess." Porter laced his fat fingers together and tipped his head thoughtfully.

"A fall from a horse, perhaps? No, that would not be likely to scrape the side of your neck. Perhaps you were struck by a woman. Or a woman's husband?" Porter raised his eyebrows and looked questioningly at Bertrand. After a moment's assessment, he shook his jowls decisively. "No, I don't think that was the case," he said.

Porter scowled and began to drum his fingers against the tabletop. It looked as though he had run out of ideas, when he spied the folded newspaper that lay half beneath the plate that held Bertrand's uneaten lunch.

"I have it!" he crowed. "You must have run into this beast, this 'Ware-Wolfe' that they've been going on about in the *Gazette!*" He snatched the paper up from the table, nearly sending the plate crashing to the floor. "I can see it now, the fearsome fanged creature and the wily Frenchman, locked in desperate battle beneath the full moon! You know," Porter winked, "John Clancy said that his dog lit into the demon and sent it packing, but perhaps that was you who dealt so soundly with the beast, eh, Bertrand?"

Jean Bertrand said nothing, but hectic patches of color had begun to form on his cheeks and his neck above the white bandage. *Let him have his fun,* he thought. *Soon he will be gone, so let him have his fun, for that's all it is.*

Porter clearly was enjoying himself. "Or, if you are not waging war against this 'Ware-Wolfe,' " he speculated, "perhaps you run in terror of it! Is that it, Bertrand? The reason you are leaving, that is? Have you been frightened away?"

"*Non!* I think not!" Bertrand spat. Porter sat back, looking oddly pleased at Bertrand's outburst.

"Good. I hope not," he said, and when he spoke, it was with a degree of unguarded sincerity. "I would expect more, even of your kind, than to believe such nonsense."

There was a moment's quiet. When Porter spoke again, he did not resume his mocking game, but the patronizing tone had returned to his voice. "Of course, you are running from something, hmm?" he said. "But I doubt that you will tell me what it is. Not that it matters..." He drained the last of his drink and set the empty mug on the table a little more loudly than necessary before continuing, "for our business is done."

Porter rose and made his way to the door once more. Bertrand followed, with a question of his own. He tried to sound cavalier.

"When, then, shall I expect..."

"Of course, the matter of payment." Porter looked irritated at having to work out the piddling details of the agreement. He pulled a slip of paper from the pocket of his coat and thrust it at Bertrand.

"This is where I live," he explained. "Come by to see me in two days' time. I should have everything ready. The papers and such, the money..." He waved a beefy hand in the air, as if to dismiss the dull topic of specifics. He pulled open the door, admitting a wedge of chilly winter air, then turned to face Bertrand. There was absolute pleasure in his face as he made his final remark.

"You know, Bertrand," he purred, "I would have paid more."

Then William Porter stepped out into the fading light, closing the door behind him, and was gone.

The relief that Bertrand felt was so laced with bitterness that he found himself unable to take any pleasure from it. There had been a time when taking such verbal abuse from the likes of William Porter would have been unthinkable. When he was younger; when he was stronger; when he was not so vulnerable and so desperate for help.

"But that was not today," he reminded himself aloud, and sank back into his chair, taking care to not aggravate his aching side.

Bertrand sat for some time, lost in a dark cloud of unpleasant thoughts. Eventually, he realized that he was staring at the newspaper, which Porter had tossed back on the table. Bertrand scolded himself for his foolishness, having left the *Gazette* out like that, in plain view. Turned to the very page, even. He shook his head in disbelief. Why had he even kept it? The article had been committed to memory days ago, every word of it, beginning with its larger-than-life headline.

INTELLIGENCE EXTRAORDINARY

Kamouraska, Dec. 2. We learn that a *Ware-Wolfe*, which has roamed through this Province for several Years, and done great Destruction in the District of Quebec, has received several considerable Attacks in the Month of October last, by different Animals, which they had armed and incensed against this Monstre; and especially, the 3d of November following, he received such a furious Blow, from a small lean Beast, that it was thought they were entirely delivered from this fatal Animal, as it some Time after retired into its Hole, to the great Satisfaction of the Public. But they have just learn'd, as the most surest Misfortune, that this Beast is not entirely destroyed, but begins again to show itself, more furious than ever, and makes terrible Havock wherever it goes.

Porter had insulted Bertrand, suggested that he was running to escape the clutches of this "Ware-Wolfe," this *loup garou*. It was ridiculous!

It was also impossible.

Bertrand smiled a little when he thought of how the smugness and certainty would melt from the Englishman's fat face if he were to know the truth. He thought of how his small eyes would protrude and how the rolls of flesh beneath his chin would quake. Bertrand was warmed by the fantasy and felt a smile touch his lips for the first time that day. For a few moments, he forgot his humiliation and his troubles.

The reprieve ended when Bertrand forgot himself and attempted to rest his feet upon the chair that Porter had left empty. Raising his leg sent searing pains from his chest to his hip. Bertrand cursed himself for being foolish and put gentle pressure on the side of his belly, the place where Clancy's dog had done its worst damage.

Bertrand winced—from the wound and from the painful reminder it served him. He had to leave. He had been exposed, to a certain degree, and he had to leave before another fierce watchdog or some zealous rifle-toting farmer ended his days. Or before another story was written for the *Gazette,* one that included his name.

Later that evening, Jean Bertrand looked out his small window and watched the pale moon rise over the treetops. From the shape of it, he knew how many good days were remaining, and he tried to mentally organize that time.

On Tuesday, he would see William Porter and collect his meager proceeds from the sale. By Friday, he imagined, he would have everything, including the animals, turned over to Porter. That left him one day, or two, at best, to be on his way. It was not much time to say goodbye to his home and his past.

Suddenly, Porter's sneering voice filled Bertrand's head. *What does it matter?* it said. *You never did well here. You never made your mark. So go.*

"I will," Bertrand whispered to himself. "I have no choice." He tried to look forward to the future, to think of it as a bright thing, but found that he could not get past his overwhelming regret. He had no children, no remaining family, no lasting business. His property was about to be divided and auctioned. Minutes after he left, there would be little to suggest that he had ever lived in this place at all. It was the cost, he supposed, of living a secret life.

Bertrand sighed and stuffed his hands into his pockets. The fingers of his right hand felt a crisply folded piece of paper there, and when he pulled it out to take a look, he heard William Porter's obnoxious voice echoing in his head, once more.

This is where I live, it said.

As Bertrand stared at the address, a revelation washed over him like a huge, shocking wave. He had no choice but to leave, that was true. But he could choose how to leave. He could run, trembling, with his tail beneath his legs, or he could show them all that he was not beaten, that years of limiting himself to poaching livestock had not entirely sapped him of his courage.

Fear, after all, was a form of respect.

It was then he decided that before he left Kamouraska, there would be time for one more visit to Porter's home. Late at night, by the cool light of *la lune*, when he was driven by the hunger and the primitive rage. For the first time in many months, Jean Bertrand found himself looking forward to something.

A change can be good, Bertrand thought, and smiled. He was starting to feel stronger already.

The article, which ran in the December 10, 1764, issue of the Quebec Gazette, closed by advising its readers to "Beware then of the Wiles of this malicious Beast, and take good Care of falling into its Claws."

The Wulver

"What do you make of it?"

Alan MacEwan was asking the question of his wife, Brenda. From the arch of her brow and the length of time she took to respond, he knew that she was baffled.

"I don't know," she finally said. "A dog? A really big dog?"

Alan shook his head and took a step back so that he could lean against the chipped Formica countertop. His wet boots made a sucking sound on the linoleum, and only then did he realize that he had come into the kitchen without taking them off. Normally, he remembered. Normally, Brenda would have yelled at him by now for having forgotten. But the two were distracted, for the moment, by something decidedly un-normal: the skull that sat gleaming on the small table of their dinette set.

"I don't think so. I've never seen a dog with a head that big, have you?"

"No," Brenda admitted. "I haven't. But how about something wild? Like a coyote, or a wolf, maybe?" She ran one finger along the smooth contours of the bleached bone and shook her head, as if dismissing her own suggestions.

The skull was huge; it took up a good portion of the tabletop. The lower jaw was missing, and the occipital bone had broken away from the rear, but still, the thing was thick and weighty. Even more curious than its size was the object's strange shape. A ridge that began between the deep eye sockets ran all the way back to the crown. The nasal bone and upper jaw were elongated, snout-like. That it was some form of beast was obvious. Exactly what type of beast was less so. All Alan MacEwan knew for certain was that this thing was not the fish he had been looking for when he had cast his line off the dock that afternoon.

Alan watched his wife examining the massive piece of bone and tried to gauge her expressions and actions. He had a theory about the skull, but he knew that Brenda would have to be in a certain state of readiness to truly hear it. She was not open-minded about things, not the way he was. Alan knew this from experience, having listened to his wife's mocking reaction every time he photographed an unidentifiable light in the evening sky or measured the impression of a suspiciously large footprint in the mud of their backyard. She said that he was a sucker, easily fooled into believing all the superstitious trash of the tabloid press. He felt that she was altogether lacking in imagination, but never said so out loud.

"I really don't know, Alan," Brenda finally said. Alan knew she truly was stymied when she added, "What do you think?" The door had been opened for Alan's opinion. He took a deep breath and offered it.

"Granddad used to tell me stories," Alan began. Brenda emitted a dismissive snort of laughter and turned back to the basket of laundry that she had been folding before he came in. Alan put his hand on her shoulder, coaxing her body to turn around until she was facing him once more. She looked at him with the condescending half smile to which he was so accustomed and started to speak. Alan raised his hand to stop her.

"Just let me finish," he said. Brenda sighed, and put her hand on her hip, striking her best make-it-quick-because-I-have-better-things-to-do pose. Alan made it quick.

"These were stories from when he was a boy, back in Scotland," Alan explained. "I've told you some of them, and I know what you think. But I never told you about the *wulver*."

Wulver. Brenda formed the word soundlessly and nodded in mock thoughtfulness. Alan ignored the bait and continued.

"Wulvers supposedly have the head of a wolf on the body of a man. They're like these wild, hybrid creatures, covered all over in thick, dark hair."

"Like a werewolf?" Brenda raised her eyebrows and Alan found himself scrambling defensively.

"Yes. No! I mean, think of a real creature that the werewolf stories might have been based on. These things, they're supposed to be reclusive, so people wouldn't ever have caught more than a glimpse of them. Supposedly, they lived in caves dug out of the hills. We've got hills around here. They, uh...they liked water! They lived on fish! I pulled this out of the *lake*, Brenda!" Alan could see that none of his arguments would convince Brenda. He forced himself to back up, to sound more reasonable and less excited.

"Look, maybe the wulver is a mythical creature, and maybe it's not," he shrugged. "I just think it's an interesting possibility. I'm curious, you know? I'd like to get this thing checked out." Alan put his hand on the top of the skull. He splayed his fingers out and found that they could not span the diameter of the relic. "Wulvers are supposed to be huge," he said, half to himself.

"This is Oregon, not Scotland," Brenda began, as she folded the last towel and placed it in the neatly packed laundry basket. "We live by a lake, not a 'loch,' and with all the campers that stampede through here in the summer, it's a

wonder we have any conventional wildlife, let alone the mythical, *reclusive* kind." She lifted the basket and balanced it on her hip, then turned to make one final point before leaving the room.

"And really, Alan," she said. "I like a few colorful folks at the family reunion as much as the next person, but your grandfather wasn't a character so much as he was a drunk." Brenda walked off in the direction of the linen closet, tossing one more comment over her shoulder as she left.

"The best part of being Scottish is the scotch, right?"

Alan said only one more thing about the skull. That evening, before he left to work his shift at the mill, he asked Brenda if she would mind him keeping the thing, temporarily, on the top shelf of the coat closet.

"I'd like to take it into town, on my days off," he explained. "I just thought that I could get the vet to take a look at it."

Brenda waved him away. "I really don't care, Alan," she said. Whatever small interest she may have had in the unusual remains had been deposed by a prime-time game show. As Alan wrapped the skull in a plastic grocery bag and stored it away above their winter coats, Brenda never took her eyes off the television screen.

Ten minutes later, as Alan followed the headlights of his pickup truck down the long, gravel drive, he felt a strange compulsion to go back and get the skull. *That's stupid*, he thought. *It's in the closet. It's safe.* He ignored the feeling and turned on to the winding road that led around the lake and up to the highway. Twenty minutes after that, he pulled into the huge paved lot and parked under the orange floodlights alongside the vehicles of a few other night-shift employees. He was still feeling uneasy, but since it was an unreasonable feeling, he simply went to work.

The porch light of the MacEwans' small bungalow had burned out, and the house was swathed in the deep shadows of trees that crept far into the yard from the surrounding woods. Puncturing the darkness, from the middle of the living room window where the drapes did not quite meet, was the flickering light of a television. A tinny sitcom laugh track bled out through the windows and doors. It was loud, loud enough that the soft crunch of gravel could barely be heard...

Brenda MacEwan had seen that episode of *Cheers* before. She had seen every episode of *Cheers* before, but there was not much else to do in the evenings when Alan was on night shift. They couldn't get cable, couldn't afford satellite, and no one wanted to come visit when it meant driving on narrow country roads in the dark. There were few friends left over from their Portland days anyway. Children would have filled the time, but there were none, despite years of trying. So Brenda watched Sam and Diane endure another lovers' spat amidst the antics of the barflies. Her mind wandered, though—partly out of boredom with the familiar plot, partly because something was vaguely bothering her.

She was bugged about the skull.

It was the sort of thing a 10-year-old boy brought home. Alan was a 37-year-old man who could be as wildly imaginative and credulous as a child, and Brenda hated to be reminded of it. She resented the way their last dollar often went toward developing shaky photos of weather balloons and that Alan often frittered away his days off running fool's errands. She knew that he'd have that stupid old bone at the vet's office on his first day off, yet there never seemed to be enough time for the odd jobs that needed tending to around the house and yard. It was nearly the end of September, and Brenda knew that she would have to nag Alan again about putting up the storm windows. The thought made her feel tired and old and alone.

Brenda sighed and punched the power button on the remote control. The television screen blinked off, and a heavy silence filled the small room. Without the distracting noise of the program, Brenda felt acutely aware of her idleness. In her mind, she considered a list of possible activities, but found herself rejecting them one by one.

It was too early for bed and she didn't feel like reading. Brenda supposed that she could write a couple of overdue letters but worried that her sour mood would spill over onto the page. The laundry was done, the house was clean, and the few dishes that had been used to serve the leftover chicken for supper were draining in the rack. There was really, truly, nothing to do, and Brenda found it dismaying.

I need a hobby, she thought. *Or an interest.* It was then that she found her gaze resting on the bi-fold door of the coat closet.

Before Brenda lifted the skull off the shelf, she carefully took note of its exact position there. Before she took it out of the plastic, she looked to see just how the bag had been wrapped and tied around it. She was curious enough to want a second look at the strange thing but felt it best that Alan not know.

The light in the kitchen was fluorescent, and it hummed in a comforting way when Brenda flipped the switch. She set the skull carefully on top of the table and then backed a couple of steps away in order to take a good, full look.

It really was bizarre. The skull was far too broad and flat at the temples to be a horse or a moose, but, Brenda was willing to admit to herself, there was no such thing as a dog of that size. As she considered the skull on the table, she ran her fingers thoughtfully over the contours of her own face and head. She felt the places where bone gave way to cartilage and muscle, felt the example of mechanical perfection where her lower jaw hinged onto the rest of her face. She tried to imagine how little room, comparatively speaking, her own skull would take up on the table.

The little kitchen window was bare, except for a stiffly ruffled valence that ran decoratively across the top. At night, when the inside lights were on and the yard was lost in a pool of inky blackness, it reflected nearly as well as a mirror. Brenda hefted the skull up off the table, held it in front of her own face, and then looked into the window glass. She had to cock her own head a bit to one side, in order to see out of one of the eye sockets, but it didn't ruin the effect. Her body was dwarfed by the massive cranium that stared ghoulishly back at her from the window.

"How big was this thing..." she whispered in wonder. As if in response to Brenda's question, her reflection appeared to move.

It was as though the image in the glass rippled, ever so slightly. Brenda brought the skull down from where she had been holding it in front of her face, so that she could see more clearly. Once more, there was movement. It looked like a shadow passing through her reflection in the windowpane.

She set the skull back on the table and leaned in close to the window. With her nose nearly pressed against the glass and her hands cupped around her face to block the light of the kitchen, she was able to see a little bit outside. Not much: between the burned-out porch light and the cloud cover, there was precious little to go by, but she could see...

A face, grotesque and hairy and inches away from her own.

Brenda screamed and recoiled so violently, she sent both of the dinette chairs crashing over on the floor. The thing outside the window roared in response, spraying saliva across the glass. Through the reflected image of the neat kitchen and her own terrified expression, Brenda caught fragments of horrifying visual information. Flashes of teeth. Blazing eyes. A broad, heavy brow and thick, black hair.

The beast tried to pass through the glass, a move that resulted in a stinging *thud* to its snout. With a loud whine, it pulled back, leaving only a broad smear of mucus. When the creature moved even inches away from the window, it became invisible in the night. *But it can see me,* Brenda realized, and fumbled for the light switch on the wall.

The kitchen went dark.

The seconds that it took for Brenda's vision to adjust were agonizingly long. When finally she was able to see, she doubted her own eyes. No more than two feet away from her kitchen window was the head of the most massive wolf she had ever seen. It was as though someone had taken the exact skull that lay on her kitchen table and padded it with flesh and fur. It was absolutely monstrous, the living version of that cranium. But the body was worse. The body appeared to be human.

The wolf-thing—*It's a wulver,* Brenda thought, *like in the stories*—had backed a step or two away from the window. She had confused the creature by turning off the light, and it was cautiously examining the frame and glass, sniffing and nudging with its wet nose. Many of the beast's gestures were feral, but its eyes were disturbingly intelligent. It even seemed eerily capable of human expression, cocking its head at one point as it noted some interesting detail.

As the wulver considered the darkened window, Brenda crouched, back pressed against the farthest wall of the kitchen, considering her options. The *thing* was outside, at least for the time being, and that was good. There was much that was bad, however. The MacEwans had a cordless phone, and Brenda could not remember where she had last set it down. The living room, maybe the bedroom. It probably didn't matter—anyone she might call was a good 20 minutes away. The closest thing to a weapon was a baseball bat that was tucked under the big queen-size bed at the opposite end of the house. And, with the truck gone, the only means of escape was a 1986 Ford Escort that only started when it was in a certain mood, and was parked 20 yards away from the back door.

The back door!

The words exploded in her head, bringing with them a fresh wave of terror. Alan never locked the back door when he left, and Brenda usually didn't bother doing so until she was about to turn in. Something that could walk erect could probably turn a doorknob. The horror of that realization jolted Brenda's body into action. She pushed herself to a standing position, slipped through the kitchen doorway, and ran down the hall. The back door tended to swell a little during wet weather, and it had been raining on and off for days. Brenda pushed against the door with all her weight and tore one fingernail down to the quick in her panic to turn the stiff deadbolt.

Brenda's momentary relief was so great, and her own pulse was beating so loudly against her eardrums, she almost didn't hear the scratching. It was whispery, tentative at first. Brenda held her breath and strained to listen.

The sound was tinny, muted and coming from the kitchen. After a moment, she realized what it was.

"Oh, God," she whispered, "it's going to tear the screen!"

As if on cue, there was a sharp metallic rip. Brenda could hear something (*paws? hands?*) thumping against the single pane of glass that remained on that side of the window. There was a pause and then a jarring symphony of crystalline high notes as the window shattered.

The wulver bellowed, and Brenda imagined that it had cut itself on the shards of glass. That would buy her a moment or two, no more. Then she would need to inflict some pain upon the beast herself, and it would have to be effective. The question was how.

The bat under the bed might as well have been a thousand miles away. Brenda wished that she had taken a knife from the block on the kitchen counter, but it was too late for that. In order to get to any other part of the house, she would have to pass the kitchen and the repulsive thing that was trying to get into it. Her only hope was to find something within arms' reach. She began a frantic search.

No matter how often Brenda tidied the back hall, it always seemed to be a mess. There were tennis shoes piled upon one another, rubber boots left to drip on the cracked plastic mat and cheap canvas slip-ons that were kept there for convenience, so that Brenda could take out the trash or make a trip to the garage without taking the time to stop for shoelaces. Every jacket and sweater in the house tended to migrate to the hooks that lined the wall, no matter how many times they were sorted into seasonal categories and hung elsewhere. The clutter always annoyed Brenda. As she tore through the mess, desperately emptying pockets in search of something, anything, *useful*, she found herself beyond annoyed. She was furious. How could there be so much stuff in one place and not a single thing that could save her life?

The thought had barely left her when she found something. Not much, but something: the black vinyl fanny pack that Brenda wore whenever she went for long walks. It contained a few essentials: a door key, tissues, sunscreen, things like that. It might do. Brenda snatched the pack off its hook and slung it around her waist like a holster. Then, quietly, she moved back down the hall toward the kitchen.

Because Brenda had already seen the wulver through the window, she thought she was ready to see it again. When she held her breath and slowly looked around the frame of the kitchen doorway, though, she discovered that she was not prepared and could never *be* prepared to see something so abhorrent trying to force its way into her home.

The beast had indeed gashed its arm quite badly on the shards of window glass. Blood was smeared on the frame, and a bright red pattern splattered across the table and continued on the linoleum. Every time the wulver moved, blood sprayed from its wound. That wasn't stopping it from moving, though.

It had managed to hoist itself halfway through the frame. From one arm, it hung from some handhold it had found on the side of the house. The other arm—which could have been human if not for the matted clumps of coarse hair—was clawing at the edge of the small table. Brenda saw that the wulver's hands were almost delicate in comparison with the rest of its being. The fingers were long and tapered, ending in either claws or long fingernails;

she could not tell which. Brenda could see what the loath-some being was trying to reach with its creepy hands, however. It was reaching for the skull.

Brenda enjoyed a moment of elation. The wulver was there for the skull, which meant that it would likely leave once it had it. But almost immediately, she realized that there was a problem. The skull was a good 18 inches beyond the beast's grasp. It swung its arm in a wide arc, leaving fresh crimson flecks marking the path, but at no point could those long fingers actually touch the bone. In order to get the skull, the wulver would have to climb through the window into the kitchen.

Brenda and Alan had lived in the house by the lake for nearly four years. They were surrounded by wilderness and encountered wildlife often enough to know that the last thing a person wanted to do was corner something wild. Animals that wandered into the yard were usually content to leave their human neighbors alone, as long as those human neigh-bors didn't back them into a place from which there was no escape. Brenda stared at the snarling, repulsive thing that was hanging through her window frame and judged that it was as much animal as it was human. It might have wanted noth-ing more than the skull at that moment, but that would change if it found itself trapped in the kitchen with her.

And that was exactly what was about to happen. The wulver had finally realized that no amount of clawing at the table was going to bring the coveted skull to within its grasp. With visible effort, it was using its wounded arm to hoist its body up and through the window frame.

Brenda whistled. In the split second that she had to for-mulate a plan, it was all that she could think of. She wanted to startle the wulver and buy herself enough time to take the half dozen steps necessary to cross the kitchen. Then, she reasoned, she could push the skull over to the edge of the table where the beast could reach it.

The wulver cringed, and its ears flattened. It raised its massive head, searching for the source of the piercing sound. It was then that Brenda realized she had made the mistake of underestimating her opponent. The vile creature's eyes locked on hers and, in an instant, she knew that whatever she was dealing with, it was not a dumb animal.

There was intelligence there. More than that, there was *intent*, something dark and malicious that came through in the intensity of that gaze. It was savage and knowing, and Brenda felt her knees weakening with fear. She might still have made it to the kitchen table, though, had it not been for what happened next.

The monster smiled.

The corners of its slick, black lips turned up ever so slightly, and Brenda could see the spittle gleaming on its enormous teeth. The effect was demonic. Brenda found herself staring stupidly at the creature's sickly twisted expression and barely noticed that the strength had gone out of her limbs. She sank to the floor, leaden with the knowledge that she was about to be killed.

The wulver was focusing entirely upon her. The skull on the table seemed forgotten as, once more, the beast poised to boost its shaggy torso further through the window. The thing grunted with effort, and a thick rope of white-flecked saliva ran out of its mouth and onto the kitchen floor. The part of Brenda's brain that was still reacting made her recoil in disgust.

*Dirty animal...I'd never let an animal in the house...no cats no dogs no nothing...*thoughts reeled through Brenda's mind, looking for purchase. As she watched the wulver pull one powerful, impossibly huge, dog-like leg through the window, one brief thought took hold. *No dogs!* her mind screamed at her. *No dogs, no dogs, no dogs!*

The fanny pack! Brenda came snapping to attention. She clutched at the black vinyl pouch that she had strapped to her waist only minutes earlier. As the wulver pulled the rest of its body through the torn screen and broken glass, Brenda ripped open the zipper. As the snarling beast poised to attack, she found the item she was looking for. She used it.

Alan MacEwan liked to sit on the edge of the loading dock while he ate his lunch. The cool night air was welcome relief from the heat and dust of the mill, and the muted sounds of night traffic on the highway soothed him. That night, however, as he began to unwrap his thick corned beef and mustard sandwiches, Alan heard something that chilled him to his marrow. It was a howl, distant but piercing and urgent, full of pain and rage. For some reason that he could not understand, Alan simply looked at his sandwiches, then refolded the plastic wrap and stuffed them back into the bag.

It had rained a little during the night, and the air was still damp and cool as Alan drove home the next morning. The truck's heater ran steadily, providing whispering accompaniment to the tinny AM radio.

Alan was accustomed to seeing his headlights bounce off the kitchen window as he turned into the yard and was surprised when they did not. It had been a cold night; it was odd that Brenda had left the window open. She was the one who folded an extra blanket over her side of the bed, even on the sweltering nights that they sometimes endured in the middle of August.

When he climbed out of the vehicle and walked toward the house, he could see more clearly that the window was not just open; the window was *gone*. Shreds of torn wire screen waved lazily in the breeze. A few jagged pieces of glass stood stubbornly in their putty, but most were missing. Alan peered through the empty space, and what he saw made wings of panic beat against his breastbone.

The table and chairs were upset, and the things that Brenda usually kept in neat order on the kitchen counter had been strewn across the floor. The sugar bowl lay broken in front of the stove, the spice rack was dangling crookedly from one nail, and the remnants of several plates littered the floor. The glass salt and pepper shakers that normally sat on a little tray above the microwave had been knocked across the room. Alan saw that the fragile neck of one of the shakers had shattered when it landed and that a white dune of salt had spilled out. *That's bad luck*, he thought, insanely. *I wonder if Brenda threw a pinch over her shoulder, ha ha.* Then he noticed all the drying reddish-brown streaks and pools on the other side of the broken window, and he stopped thinking at all. Alan ran for the back door and started screaming his wife's name before he even managed to fit the key in the lock.

The house had been destroyed. Alan ran from room to room, calling out to Brenda and noting each terrible detail with fresh horror. The back of the sofa had been slashed, and stuffing was bursting from the wounded fabric like soft, beige entrails. Deep scratches were dug into the wooden top of the coffee table, as though someone had dragged a rake across its surface. Books and knick-knacks were everywhere, some broken and torn, others simply toppled from their places upon the shelves. The mirror that hung over the table by the hall had been struck by something heavy. It bore a scar-like circle of crushed glass, the epicenter of damage from which a road map of cracks had spread. Just beyond that, in the hallway, a ragged hole had been punched in the drywall.

There was a stench in the house, too, something sharp and vile and choking. Alan gagged once or twice and felt his eyes stinging and tearing in response to the pollution. *What in God's name was here?* he thought in the midst of his frenzied search.

Alan finally found Brenda in the bedroom. She was in a small, crumpled heap behind the closet door, which had been torn nearly off its tracks. Her knees were pulled up to her chest, and her arms were wound tightly around them. Alan could see deep scratches that went from her elbows to her wrists (*like the coffee table,* he thought). Her jeans had been torn along the seam by her left hip, and a dark patch of blood had soaked through.

Brenda had her face hidden in the cocoon of her limbs, and at first, Alan didn't know if she was dead or alive. There was no movement, no obvious breathing, no sign that she was aware of his presence. Alan heard his own voice, unnaturally shaky and high-pitched, calling her.

"Brenda?"

Slowly, she raised her head. There was a puffy purple

bruise rising on one cheekbone, and a gash on her forehead. Her eyes were bloodshot and watery. Her bottom lip was split and swollen, and when she first tried to speak, she winced and raised a hand to gently touch the corner of her mouth. Alan pushed the broken door aside and knelt down next to her.

"Brenda, what happened?"

When she spoke, even her voice sounded pained.

"We have to go down to the lake," was all she said.

Alan helped her to her feet, and it was then he saw that she had been clutching something to her chest. It was a small spray canister. Alan recognized part of a cartoon logo of a vicious German shepherd and knew that the words below its snarling muzzle were "Dog-Gone." It was pepper spray. The canister was empty, but the tip of Brenda's index finger, white with pressure, remained firmly pressed on the nozzle. When he tried to take it from her, she refused to let go.

On the way out of the house, Brenda stopped in the ruined kitchen. She gestured weakly in the direction of the floor-to-ceiling shelves that Alan had built during his last vacation.

"It got knocked under there," she said. "When the table tipped."

Alan crouched down to look. In the tight space between the floor and the lowest shelf, he could see a little puff of dust, a wayward twist-tie, and a glimpse of smooth white bone. He tugged at it and found it would not budge. Down on his hands and knees, he took a closer look and saw that one of the eye sockets had become firmly hooked on a loose bracket. Alan pried the shelf up and was able to free the skull that was trapped beneath. When he pulled it out, Brenda simply nodded.

"Bring it," she said.

Ten minutes later, the two stood at the end of the dock. Alan hefted the skull in his hands a few times, judging the weight of it and the strength of his pitching arm.

"Are you sure you want to do this?" he asked. "It's our only proof, you know."

Brenda had to look at Alan to be certain that he was teasing. She saw the little smile on his face and knew that he was.

"We could be on TV," he coaxed, and playfully held the skull up in front of his own face.

Brenda went pale. The bruises on her face stood out in sharp contrast to her ashen complexion, and Alan cringed at his own insensitivity.

"Just throw it," she said, and he did.

The skull hit with a tremendous splash, sending up a silver spray of water that reflected the morning sun. As it sank below the surface, Alan shouted out across the still water.

"*We're giving this back!*" he roared. A loon called out an answer, and then the quiet descended once more.

The two stood for several minutes, staring across the lake to the rolling hills dressed in their warm autumn colors. Finally, Alan turned to Brenda. He could see that some of the tension had already drained out of her face.

"You know," he said, "I'll never be famous, now. And no one will ever believe me."

Brenda smirked as much as her injured mouth would allow.

"Fame is overrated," she said. "And from now on, I'll believe you. Let's go home."

Brenda took Alan's hand as they walked down the dock toward the parked truck. "I'll tell you the whole story, now," she said, "and we'll see if you believe *me*."

"You know I will," he smiled. "I'm a sucker for that kind of stuff."

According to an article by Dr. Karl P.N. Shuker in the November 2000 issue of FATE *magazine, the people who originally reported this experience said that returning the strange skull to the lake seemed to create peace. The terrifying creature thought to be a "wulver" never again visited the little house in search of its ancestor's remains.*

The Strangest Thing

"What's the strangest thing you've ever seen?" Paul asked, then sank into the easy chair opposite Marian and set two glasses and a bottle of merlot on the table between them.

"The strangest thing..." she mused, and leaned back comfortably into the cushions of her own chair while Paul filled her glass. She considered the question carefully, for there was no such thing as small talk between the two friends. What continued to bring them together, in spite of increasingly demanding schedules and family obligations, was their mutual appreciation for good conversation in general and good storytelling in particular.

"I could tell you about a guy I used to date when I was in college, but that wouldn't be entirely dignified," she winked, and took a sip of wine. It was an inside joke. Marian and Paul had dated briefly, in college, before they discovered that it was their friendship and not their romance that held true potential.

Paul chuckled but said nothing. Marian saw that he was still wearing a look of great anticipation. It didn't surprise her. When Paul asked for a story, he truly expected—or at least hoped—to hear a good one. It always made her want to impress him. And given the question of the evening, she thought she probably would. She had known immediately what her answer to his question would be; there would be no matter of comparing experiences and making judgments. Marian Buckley had a fantastic story about the strangest thing that she had ever seen, and she relished the thought of telling it.

"It happened back in the mid-60s," she began. "Remember Buddy, my first husband? He was a truck driver, and he'd gotten a job at an asbestos mine in northern B.C. We were just married, no kids, and there was nothing for me to do up there. I mean *nothing*..."

Marian would always remember the steady decline of her mood during that first week of living in the little mining community. On day one, she discovered that her depressingly cramped little house was one of a hundred identical units in the camp-owned town, and she lost all interest in sprucing it up. On day two, she unpacked her small television set—a wedding gift from her mother—and learned that there was no reception of any kind in their remote pocket of mountains. On day three, she listened to the nearest radio station capable of casting a signal over the rocky peaks and grew weary of the twangy country standards it played by noon. That evening, as they ate macaroni and cheese off their brand-new turquoise Pyrex plates, Marian told Buddy that she was thinking of taking up a hobby. Buddy nodded, belched and asked for seconds, establishing a style of communication that would eventually doom their marriage to a brief, three-year run.

Marian settled upon sketching. She liked to draw, and for the price of some charcoal and a pad of paper, she could begin. All that she needed was subject matter, but finding that was more difficult than she imagined.

Still life bored her; all those bowls of waxy fruit and vases of blossoms were uninspiring. Portraiture seemed an unlikely choice, as she didn't know anyone well enough to ask them to pose. Marian was left with the option of landscape artistry, and so she began to set out on regular morning hikes, her sketch pad under her arm, searching for examples of rugged beauty among the faded, dried-out pines that forested her remote and rocky surroundings.

She found one location that worked particularly well. Getting there required a 20-minute walk along an abandoned mine access road. The rough gravel trail twisted and turned along the side of one mountain, ending in a plateau-like turnaround that overlooked the little camp town. The distance was nearly sufficient to make the drab cluster of weathered houses and utilitarian community buildings appear picturesque, so Marian chose the plateau as her regular sketching spot.

Daily, she visited the desolate place and tried to capture the scenery on her paper. She went there in the early morning, when the sun had just risen above the highest peak, and the valley was awash in fresh, white light. She sometimes sketched in the afternoon, when the narrow streets were active with the wives she hadn't yet bothered to meet and their pale, isolated children. At some point, Marian decided that it was necessary to see her vista in the evening, when the sun was behind her back, casting long shadows across the town.

She told Buddy, and he seemed enthusiastic.

"That's good," he said, "good idea," and for a moment, Marian was pleased that he was showing interest in what she was doing. She was just about to ask him to join her when he said, "A few of the single guys from the bunkhouses, they're having a little beer bash tomorrow. If you've got something of your own to do, I won't worry about getting home too early."

The plan was made, and the next evening, Marian found herself shivering in the chill of twilight, watching as darkness descended upon her ugly little town. She was in a foul mood, distracted by the cold and by her annoyance with Buddy, and she wasted several clean sheets of sketch paper trying to capture the eerie quality of nightfall upon the bleak scenery. It seemed impossible and, finally, she closed her pad and put away her pencils.

Marian zipped up the canvas bag she used to carry her materials and rose from the large, smooth rock that served as her daily perch. Then she turned back toward to the road and sucked her breath in sharply when she saw that she was not alone.

The coarse gravel that lay on the rutted road gave way to something more akin to rubble along the shoulders. Closer to the sheer rock face of the mountain, the rubble turned into large, broken boulders. Some were as tall as a man, and it was beside one of these huge rocks, hidden in the deep blue shade, that Marian saw someone. From the size and shape of the silhouette, she judged it to be a man, but the stranger's features were well hidden in the gloom. The stillness of his pose and the direction he appeared to be facing made it quite clear that he was watching her.

Twenty minutes from town. Completely alone. Unarmed. No one at home to notice if she was late. The thoughts ran rapid-fire through Marian's head while she bent over to tie her shoelace and tried to appear entirely calm. *And why shouldn't I be calm?* she asked herself. After all, the man hadn't threatened her in any way. He was probably from town, just out for a walk, just one of the locals she hadn't yet met. Marian decided that she had come upon a good time to end her antisocial streak and called out in a friendly voice.

"Hi there! Would you happen to know what time it is?"

Her query was met with silence, and within seconds, Marian progressed from being nervous and uncomfortable to being purely afraid. There was nothing to do but start walking, though, so she picked up her bag and started across the broad plateau in the direction of the road.

Marian had to walk past the character lurking in the shadows in order to get back on the winding little road. As she did so, she maintained the greatest distance possible without appearing obviously afraid and took the opportunity to sneak a few sideways glances at the stranger from a closer vantage point. She was able to detect the shaggy outline of a beard and saw that the man was taller and heavier than she had first thought. His facial features, however, remained well hidden in the deepening shadows. With the sun completely behind the mountain, the light had begun to fade quickly. Marian realized that it would not be long before the road itself would be hidden in darkness, and she quickened her pace.

Marian moved along smartly, but she did not run. Instinctively, that seemed important to her, that she not break into a run and force whoever was following her to give chase. And she was quite certain that she was being followed: she could feel eyes and attention focused sharply upon the back of her neck, where the fine, sensitive hairs stood on end. At one point, she heard a footstep that was not her own; the grinding sound of gravel caught underfoot, and before she had taken a moment to consider whether it was wise to do so, she turned.

The large, dark figure was trailing her by no more than a few steps.

Marian felt cold shock sweep through her. She stumbled once but kept herself from falling and managed to resume her quick pace. Suddenly, it had become difficult to stop herself from running, difficult to keep from panicking. She was at least 10 minutes away from safety, and the person behind her was no longer bothering to walk quietly...

As panic gripped Marian's mind, some cool, detached voice within her made a suggestion. *If you're going to be attacked,* it said, *have it happen on your own terms.* The thought gave her strength that she had not known she had, courage enough to spin around and confront her stalker.

"What the hell do you want?!" she demanded. Then, in the thin, silver light of the moon that had just begun to rise, Marian saw her pursuer for the first time, and her voice left her.

Though it was roughly the shape and size of a man, it could only be described as a beast. Long, tangled clumps of dirty fur framed a face made up of brutish features. The eyes burned with animal rage; the nose had the long, flat appearance of a canine snout. The mouth would have been more aptly described as a muzzle, and when it parted, Marian could see rows of powerful, knife-like teeth. It was horrible; it was absolutely fearsome. Then, suddenly, the creature was crouching with its powerful, clawed fingers outstretched, and Marian knew that it was about to pounce.

The canvas bag lay in the gravel, several steps away. Marian had dropped it when she first saw the wolf-beast. She was left with nothing at her disposal but the clothing she wore and the one item that she had tucked into her jacket pocket before leaving the house: a small flashlight. Marian had anticipated needing the light during the dark walk home. She had been right.

She grabbed the little light and wielded it in the monster's face. "Leave me alone!" she screamed, as she snapped on the switch.

The yellow beam of light struck the beast squarely in its eyes. Temporarily blinded, it yelped in pain and raised one arm to protectively cover its face. It was then that Marian saw the shredded cloth, the remnants of a shirt cuff that remained buttoned around one shaggy animal wrist. The effect was loathsome, simply *wrong*. Marian could feel sour, acidic revulsion rising up in her throat.

"What *are* you?" she whispered. She would never receive an answer. Quite suddenly, before the glare of the flashlight, the wolf-like creature vanished. It happened so abruptly, Marian gasped in shock and then spun about in a circle, expecting to find that the beast had ducked behind her. She found that she was quite alone on the dark gravel road, brandishing the flashlight like a weapon and listening to the ragged sounds of her own breath.

"Are you *serious?*"

Marian had to smile a little when she looked at Paul. He was sitting, quite literally, on the edge of his seat, his comfortable cushions abandoned and his wine glass forgotten in front of him. She nodded, indicating that she was quite serious, and he shook his head in wonderment.

"What did you *do?*" he asked. Marian shrugged.

"I went home," she answered simply. "I went to bed. I gave up sketching."

"That *can't* be the end of the story," Paul pleaded, and his expression was so desperate that Marian could not keep herself from laughing aloud. It was a rare pleasure to have her cynical friend so engrossed in one of her stories, and she decided that it was wicked to tease him.

"No, it's not quite the end of the story," Marian said, and her voice was again serious. "I never told Buddy about what happened—he would have had me committed. But eventually, I made a couple of friends up there. One of them had lived in the town for years and years. Her husband was this kind of bigwig at the mine. But she was alright, you know? I trusted her. So one day I told her about my little adventure." Marian paused to sip her wine.

"And?" Paul urged.

"And she told me an interesting story in turn," said Marian, and she set aside her glass and leaned forward until she and Paul were only inches apart. "She said that she knew why that little access road had been abandoned. She said that when they were grading it, they unearthed a shallow grave that held some very strange remains. The body of the skeleton looked like a human being, but the head...the head appeared to be a wolf." Marian raised her eyebrows and leaned back in her chair once more. "She said that afterward, there were a few accidents at that exact point on the road, and that it wasn't too long before the company brass decided to close that little stretch of gravel in favor of another route."

"Wow," Paul breathed, and sank back into his chair. After a few moments, he looked up at Marian and raised on eyebrow questioningly. "True story?" he asked.

"Well," she responded, "I can only vouch for my part of it, for what I saw, but, yeah, true story."

"And after all these years," said Paul, "what do you think it was that you saw? A ghost? A werewolf?"

"Yes," said Marian, and she smiled, knowing that she had told the best story of the evening.

The true tale upon which this story is based can be found in Stefan Elg's 1967 book, Beyond Belief *(Tower Publications). Elg describes the woman involved as being "thoroughly unsuperstitious" at the time of her strange encounter and wondered whether skepticism actually helps people to survive such terrifying experiences. Whether that is so remains to be proven, but the woman's practical nature surely made her a more credible witness.*

Part Three

Vampires

For most people, the word "vampire" conjures images of Dracula, the character created by author Bram Stoker in his novel of the same name. While it is true that much of the modern vampire myth is owed to Stoker's fertile imagination, vampires existed in Eastern European folklore for hundreds of years before the Transylvanian count made his first appearance.

In medieval times, people often created myths to help them explain and cope with the horrors of daily life. Outbreaks of disease, terrible slaughters and fears (not altogether unfounded) of being buried prematurely were all dealt with through stories of vampirism. In that time, the vampire was considered a bloodthirsty monster that inspired only fear and revulsion.

Since the publication of Stoker's incredibly popular book, vampires have evolved into creatures that are often more titillating than terrifying. Today's popular culture gives us sensuous-looking *vampires that elicit a variety of emotional responses. The fear still exists, but now it may be mixed with desire, sympathy and even envy.*

Beneath the newly glamorous exterior, however, there remains a core of evil. Today's vampire may be wearing Dracula's stylish, satin-lined cape, but he is afflicted with the ugliest of curses, possesses an unquenchable thirst for blood and is always seeking another soulless, undead creature to keep him company...

Us.

It's 4 AM, and there is a lull here.

That's usual. I've been working the night shift at this 24-Hour Mart for five years now, selling chocolate bars and lotto tickets and heating sub sandwiches for stoners with the munchies, and there is almost always a lull at 4 AM.

Most of the bars and clubs have been closed for an hour by that time, and an hour is long enough for the people to pick up their cigarettes and their snacks and go home. The kids, the Marilyn Manson wanna-bes with their black lipstick and pierced faces, they get tired of playing the video games and hanging around the parking lot by about midnight, or one. They're gone, too.

At 4 AM, most of the ones you'll see in here are Us.

I've washed down the slush machine and restocked the cooler, so I have a little time to myself. I've been skimming through a paperback from one of the cheap wire racks, just for laughs. I pick it up and settle down to read for a few minutes.

It's a vampire story. The cover is predictably lurid, and vampire is spelled with a "y," for the sake of flair. Inside, it's all the usual stuff. High drama and style, you know, with the Stoker-inspired capes and coffins full of graveyard dirt. Me, I sleep on a queen-size waterbed with a slow leak, in a cramped bedroom with industrial-strength black garbage bags taped over the windows.

Vampyres. This guy wrote a whole book, and he probably thinks he never met one.

The buzzer above the door squawks, announcing an

arrival. It always seems louder in the middle of the night when there are few other sounds. The guy who walks in is Us. I haven't seen him before, but I can tell right away. If you wonder how, you're assuming I struggle with the same five pale senses that you have.

The guy buys a pack of spearmint gum and a *People* magazine. He puts his change in the UNICEF box and leaves, with the magazine rolled under his arm and the gum stuffed into the breast pocket of his worn denim jacket. He looks like one of the graveyard workers from the nearby industrial park. There are lots of Us over there.

The nighttime disc jockey on the oldies radio station that I listen to—I've heard that he is Us. Of course, you can't tell by voice alone, but it's a good bet. He's been there for years, doing the same shift, and he always sounds tired. I know what that's about—being tired. You can dismiss it as "shift-work syndrome," but, really, lethargy is just a part of Us. It just goes with the territory.

A lot of the hookers are Us. And quite a few night watchmen. The driver who takes the number 42 bus past here every night—he is. So is Andrew, the bartender at an after-hours club called "The Plum Tomato." It's a gay hangout and, even though Andrew's been there for three years, he says it still amazes him. When he was a kid, they used to burn queers and witches at the stake.

I wait on a sleepy woman who buys a bottle of cherry red cough syrup. She says her kid has a cold and can't sleep. I commiserate and count out her change. She is not Us, and I can feel her pulse like a drum on my skin.

I tell her, "Be careful you don't catch that bug yourself," and she gives me a tired smile as she leaves. I feel insincere, because I know that she already has it. She won't know for two or three days.

I go back to my book. Reading it makes me wish that, like the fictional count, I could have a "familiar" to take care of all the mundane necessities of life. Or, at least, the vacuuming. I'd also like to sign up for the wardrobe—very stylish, according to this author and most others who write in the genre. Of course, after five years, any outfit that doesn't involve ketchup-repellent polyester and a combination pocket protector/name tag sounds dapper to me.

The buzzer wails again, and here's someone else invading my treasured 4 AM lull. I look up from the book and see that I know her. Well, a little, anyway. She's a prostitute who calls herself Terry. Her real name is Edith, and it has been for over 100 years.

Terry wears a lot of bright, greasy makeup and teases her brown hair out like a lion's mane. I think she would look better, prettier, without the getup, but Terry needs the hair, the glitter shadow, the heels and the leather mini to look older. She changed when she was 17. Now, she's eternally 17 and, like a lot of the young girls who are Us, not old enough to hold down a legal job that keeps her out all night. I sometimes bemoan the fact that I am 20, forever gangly and awkward, forever with the hated red scars of recent acne mapped across my pale face. But I can work. I can drive a car. Some of the kids who are Us, they can't make it, even with good fake I.D.

So, in runs Terry, in such a crazy hurry that she nearly takes out a stand of creme-filled cupcakes. But it's not her frantic entrance that startles me, really. It's her fear.

Fear is like perspiration on most people. You can smell

it on someone—that's no joke. I can sense it on Terry now; it's seeping from her pores and whooshing out of her lungs. There are the bright panic lights in her eyes, too, and her breath is short and rapid, as if she has run a distance. There's something dark smeared on her chin and on the front of her cheap, clingy sweater. Her teeth are showing a little.

"Help me, James!" she pants. "Please! I killed a guy!"

Now, if I'm not mistaken, you probably have an idea about Us, about what we are and how we live. But, believe me, you've been stuffed with lies and garbage from movies and bad paperbacks, like the one I set aside as Terry staggers toward my counter. And so, you're thinking *of course she killed someone.* You expected it. But you're wrong.

It's been more than a dozen years since there was a human death in this city that could be blamed on one of Us. That was unfortunate. It was ugly. Without getting too specific, I can say that it involved a street person and an overzealous, misinformed, new member. But it was an "isolated incident," as they say. For the most part, we're a lot less violent than the human population. Believe me. We learned a long time ago that it was safer to live quietly and maintain a sense of civilization.

Of course, I understand how some of the stories get started; there's a grain of truth in most things. The sunlight, for example. It makes Us uncomfortable, and even ill, after a long enough time—but we don't turn to a pile of ash and bone. I live by night—we all do—but there are still some bits of business that have to be done by daylight hours. I'm careful, that's all. I dress for coverage; I wear sunscreen; I hope for clouds. When I get back home, I stretch out on my couch for a couple of hours, feeling as though I have a low-grade flu.

My point is that there is *something*, some basis to the idea that sunlight harms Us. And there's *something* to the feeding legends. Sure, we need blood to sustain us. But I don't go stalking my dinner any more than you do. I mean, we've *all* evolved, right?

I make do with a couple of birds each week. Sometimes a stray cat. I have a friend who raises mice in her cellar. She has me over for dinner once in a while, and they're delicious. I know a couple of Us who have been to "feeding circles," taking advantage of some of the freaks and Goths and role players who are more than happy to let you suck at their wrists for a thrill. I never tried it. I don't like those sorts of people and, besides, the mere thought of drinking from a human being tickles my gag reflex.

So, like I was saying, we're *not* murderers. The fact that you would believe us to be so necessitates a large measure of discretion in our everyday lives. Even one questionable death could threaten our entire community—and now Terry is telling me, wild-eyed, that she has killed a man.

There's nobody else in the place, no one even in the parking lot, under the wide arcs of fluorescent light. That's good, because Terry's looking absolutely hysterical. There's strange, hectic color in her face, and she's waving her arms around madly, and anyone who saw her would bring the cops running. Before some stranger does come in and see her, I coax her into the back, into the cramped little staff room with the chipped Formica table and folding metal chairs.

"Sit down," I say. "Have one of your cigarettes." I can see that she has some; there's a crumpled package falling out of the pocket of her cheap, fringed, vinyl coat. There are a lot of Us with the habit; after all, immortality is a good defense for most of the anti-smoking arguments. Still, the cost is enough to keep me away.

I quickly check the front and when I come back, Terry's trying to light her smoke. She's shaking like she has some severe palsy, so I cup my hands around hers to steady the flame until it takes.

Her skin is warm.

Remember I said that we're often tired? I should add that we are always cold. My mother was fond of saying that every November, a chill would settle into her bones, and it would not leave until there were buds on the trees in May. Of course, body temperature has nothing to do with the bones. It's the blood—which is likely why the small relief that we enjoy comes after some nourishment.

That feeling is like a glow, a minor, temporary rise in temperature. What I feel in Terry's hands, though, that's different. It's *heat*; it's fever; it's something alive, beneath her skin.

I move back to the doorway, where I can watch the store, and I ask her what happened.

"Stupid *idiot!*" she spits, then fills her lungs with a long, intense drag. I don't think she means me, so I don't react.

"He got *himself* killed!" she says. "I didn't know what else to do!"

Terry gets up and starts pacing. She's more in control now, surprisingly energetic in fact, and she tells me about a john that she had early in the evening. He tried to take his

money back after the trick. He said she wasn't worth $50—
Terry's eyes flash when she tells me this—and he started to
slap her around a bit.

Now, Terry works for a guy, a big jerk of a human
named Ozzie, and when he heard the commotion, he came
upstairs and tossed the john out in the alley. Ozzie shoved
Terry around some, too, just for good measure. The rest of
the night was business as usual.

"But I guess he stayed outside and waited," she says,
chewing on one long, electric blue fingernail, "because
when I started out for home this morning, he followed."

"I wasn't worried, you know. In fact, it was funny." She
doesn't say why, but I know what she means. I can imagine
this sad jerk, crawling through filth behind the dumpsters
and ducking in and out of the shadows that bleed between
parked cars, all because he's stealthily stalking Terry, who
can see him like it's daylight and feel his heartbeat and
swelling lungs like she has a stethoscope mashed into his
flabby chest. It would have been funny, except that—Terry's
telling me this, now—he decided to attack her.

She lights another cigarette; this time with steady hands
(warm hands...). Then she tells me the worst part.

"I was half a block away," she says, "and thinking that
I'd come and see you for a while, if I couldn't shake this
creep. That's when he took a run at me." Terry stops and
shakes her head. "I heard him coming, so I turned
around. And he looked crazy, James, you know? Red-
faced, glassy-eyed. He had these big, meaty hands, and he
was holding them straight out in front of him, with his
fingers curled like claws. So I turned and tried to run. But
he grabbed my jacket."

Terry turns, so I can see. The white vinyl is smeared from the right shoulder down. Five grimy finger trails end in a torn patch of fringe, right above the small of Terry's back. The creep might have gone home with no more than a handful of synthetic fringe, except, Terry tells me, she lost her footing then. I look at her feet, and I can see why. She's wearing 4-inch plastic platforms. Her toenails are painted in the same shocking blue shade as her fingernails.

"So I fell down," she says, "and I guess he figured on getting his 50 bucks worth then, because when I hit the pavement, he was right there. He had my arms pinned up above my head..." Terry sort of drifts off, like she doesn't want to talk about it anymore. I don't want to talk about it either, but it's important.

"What happened?" I ask, even though I know. Terry did what she had to do.

"I got his throat," she whispers, sounding almost dreamy. "I mean, I sunk in. Got hold of him and started drinking. He went nuts, trying to pull away, making this weird, freaking noise. He flipped over on his back, and I went with him. Still hanging on. But I was getting so full; I mean, who *ever* gets to drink that much, you know? I didn't want to puke it all up, so I pulled out. He got a good look at me then, and I know my teeth were showing."

Terry paused for a minute, and I finally had to ask her.

"So, did you?..."

"No." She says and stubs out the butt of her smoke in the bent tin ashtray that sits on the staff room table. "I didn't have to. Not technically, anyway. He had a heart attack. I felt it. His face twisted up, and his eyes were bulging, and I felt his heart just...blow."

Terry waves her hands in a wide circle, palms outward, to illustrate. I get the picture, but the drama of the pervert's heart attack is lost on me. As I watch Terry move around the little room like an energetic cat, eyes bright, skin still flushed warm, I can think of only one thing.

"You drank him..." I mumble, almost to myself.

Her eyes flick away for a moment, and I know that she feels ashamed.

"I had to do it. I had no choice," she says, defensively. "And it's not like they say, James, not at all."

The buzzer over the door goes off. It seems far away, but I hear it. I stand up and point to the employee washroom, where she can wash away the blood that stains her face and clothing. Then I turn and walk out into the store, and I hear Terry say, to no one in particular, "It was good..."

The guy who comes in the store is the first of my morning regulars. He's a cab driver who comes in every day at this time for a java and a paper. I haven't even made fresh coffee yet, and I apologize for making him wait. He says it's okay, gonna be a bitch of a morning to drive anyway, the way the rain's starting.

I hear the rain, coming down on the store's flat tar roof. And I hear water running from the rusty pipes in the back washroom, rinsing everything away.

It's been 18 hours.

I had trouble sleeping today; felt a little undernourished. The hamster I bought at the mall pet store on my evening off wasn't as juicy as it looked. Not satisfying at all, even though my appetite this morning had surely been curbed by the events last night.

I see on the evening news that the police have found the pervert. The steady rain had washed him pretty clean. They haven't yet determined the cause of death, and the autopsy is scheduled for Thursday.

"There are no suspects at this time," the announcer says, and I get a pretty good picture of the cops, drinking coffee out of Styrofoam cups, saying, "What would do that? An animal? A knife of some kind? What?" They'll close the file, eventually, but Terry got on a Greyhound tonight anyway.

She's going back East, she says, and I think it's just as well. When she got cleaned up, she looked really good, you know. Healthy. Ready for a fresh start. If that fat pimp Ozzie doesn't track her down, I think she'll be fine.

I'm walking to work, taking a bit of a detour, feeling tired and *feeling tired* of feeling tired, if you know what I mean. There's still a drizzle coming down, and the chill is biting in deep. I'm shivering, and I can't help thinking of Terry, last night, with that heat under her skin and that vitality in her eyes. I'm wondering what civilization gives you, for what it takes away.

I come to a crumbling brick apartment house, the purpose of my detour, and I step back from the street, placing myself quietly in the shadows.

There's a newspaper box a few yards away, and as I wait patiently in the dark, I read the headline. "INNER CITY SLASHING!" it says tonight. I wonder what it will say tomorrow.

I hear heavy footsteps now, coming down the stairs of the apartment, approaching the side door. I tune in physically. I'm both pleased to find that it is who I am waiting for and repulsed to be sensually connected to such filth.

The door swings open, releasing a wedge of yellow light into the alley, and Ozzie steps out. I feel my lips beginning to draw back as I move from the shadows.

I have to try it, just once.

It might be good for Us.

Those who report on vampire culture today usually note that there are a number of distinctive groups within it.

There are those who are role players, or "lifestylers," who dress in stereotypical black costumes and frequent neo-Gothic clubs or other realms of fantasy. They may have a taste for drinking blood but have no physical need for it.

There are those who believe that they were "born" vampires, the "sanguinarians" who feel a physical need to consume blood, although they often shun the popularized images of vampirism. Some of these people may suffer from porphyria, a rare blood disease that causes extreme sensitivity to sunlight, excessive hair growth and tightening of the skin around the lips and gums, making the teeth more prominent.

There are self-professed "psychic vampires," who say that they feed not upon the blood, but upon the energy of their unsuspecting victims.

Finally, there are those who claim that they are the vampires of legend: immortal and ageless, with an insatiable hunger for blood and the ability to create others like them.

Do the legendary vampires truly exist? In our 24-hour culture, where lives can be lived entirely after the sun has set, it is easy to imagine that a legion of such creatures is existing quietly in our midst...

The Woman

The official reception that had been organized to mark the opening night of the play had been rather luxurious. Servants circulated trays of delectable hors d'oeuvres, and the guests sipped on a surprisingly good wine said to have survived the Great War in the director's cellar. By contrast, the impromptu gathering to which a number of the actors and younger guests repaired later on was the sort where people poured cheap spirits into chipped, mismatched cups and gave no thought to food.

The dark-haired young man attended both soirees. He had been impressed by the first but felt that the second held more promise in terms of fulfilling his personal ambitions.

He arrived alone but hoped that he would not leave that way. There had been a woman at the reception—a beautiful, delicate, blonde creature—whom he had hoped to meet. Before a proper opportunity had presented itself, however, she had been whisked away. After a few discreet inquiries, the young man learned of the "after" party. He solicited the address from a half-drunk costumer and walked several blocks to one of Budapest's verging-on-shabby districts, which featured row after row of buildings that formed a honeycomb of rented rooms and flats. Once he had turned onto the street, he could have found the apartment without knowing its exact number, for the gathering had already grown boisterously loud.

The young man climbed toward the second-floor rooms in a shadowy stairwell that was lit by a single, naked, yellow bulb. As he drew closer to the party, he began to choke on the smell of cigarettes. Even the hall outside the apartment had begun to fill with a suffocating blue haze.

He stood at the door for a moment, wondering whether he should knock. It was likely that no one would hear him above the din of conversation and laughter, and it would therefore be pointless. Furthermore, knocking at the door—if he *was* heard—might only draw attention to the fact that he had not actually been invited. The young man decided that the best course of action was to simply apply a mask of confidence and walk in. The instant he did so, he felt foolish for having spent so much time and care on his approach. No one bothered to even turn and acknowledge that there was a new arrival.

The flat was essentially one moderate-sized room, which had been divided into two smaller areas through the strategic placement of furniture. One side appeared to be the kitchen. There was a small counter and basin and, above that, an open cupboard which held a few essential plates and bowls, a couple of small tins and a box of crackers. The other side of the room was a living area, made comfortable with some mismatched chairs, a colorful, woven wall hanging and shelves stuffed full of books. It was difficult to see more than that, for the place held a shoulder-to-shoulder crowd of revelers.

Had it not been for several familiar faces, the young man would not have guessed that the apartment party had evolved from the formal opening-night reception. It seemed too raucous to be the same group. There were men telling bawdy stories and women rewarding them with brittle, too-loud laughter. There were actors, still in heavy stage makeup, offering impromptu performances of their favorite lines, and overdressed patrons who applauded them vigorously. There was a song being sung over in one corner and a competing melody starting up nearby. One daring couple was kissing, their arms wound around one another and their eyes closed to create the privacy they desired. And near the counter, with its little ceramic wash basin, political opinions that no one would have dared to whisper at the public party were being shouted out in the course of heated debate.

The young man saw all this as he scanned the crowd, but he did not see whom he had come to see: the lovely, pale blonde in the shimmering red dress.

"I must say, you appear lost."

The voice was feminine and teasing, and the young man turned around with a tremendous sense of anticipation. The woman who stood smiling behind him, though, was short and square, with masses of dark, frizzy ringlets framing her face. The young man tried unsuccessfully to conceal his disappointment.

The woman laughed.

"So you are *not* here to see me," she said. "Well, we knew that."

The young man realized that he had not yet spoken a word and that the moment for a simple "hello" had passed. He reached into his arsenal of polite conversation and selected something appropriate.

"Were you at the reception?" he asked, in a pleasant tone.

"For a short time, yes," the dark woman nodded. "I was with her."

"With whom?"

"With *her*." When the young man still appeared confused, the dark woman smiled, closed her eyes and shook her head, as though frustrated with a very thick-headed student. When she spoke again, it was slowly and deliberately, with careful emphasis on each word.

"The one you're looking for," she said. "The one who is here, waiting for you now."

"Not the beautiful blonde!?" The question was out before the young man had time to consider its appropriateness.

"Aha! He *does* know!" the dark woman laughed. "Yes, the blonde. Do you wish to meet her, now?"

The young man was stunned at his good fortune.

"I...ah, yes. Very much so, please," he stammered.

The dark woman motioned for the young man to follow her as she squeezed her way through the crowd. Together, they maneuvered across the room, pressing past unfamiliar bodies that smelled of perspiration and perfume and alcohol. They went as far as the opposite wall, where the young man was surprised to find that they were standing in front of a door. He had scanned the room only minutes earlier and had not noticed a door.

"With so many people, it is difficult to see," said the dark woman. The comment struck the young man as being eerily accurate, until he realized that it was no more than a casual remark given meaning by coincidental timing.

The door opened then, and the young man walked through. He heard the latch click shut. The sounds of the party became suddenly muted. He turned to speak to the dark woman and saw then that she had not followed him. For a moment, he thought he had been locked in a dark little room, all alone, as some sort of joke. Then his eyes began to adjust to the dim light, and the young man saw that he was not alone at all.

The woman was sitting in an upholstered chair beside a bed that had the coverlet thrown back, revealing crisp, white linens. By the flickering light of a candelabra that sat in an alcove above the head of the bed, the young man could see that she was still wearing the crimson gown that flattered her figure so well. Her hair fell to her shoulders in platinum waves, and her lips, pressed together in a small smile, matched the vibrant shade of her dress.

The young man nearly swooned at the sight of her, but this time did not miss the moment of greeting.

"Hello," he said. He had the benefit of some vocal training and employed every method he knew to make himself sound masculine and assured.

"Hello."

It was the first time he had heard her speak. The woman's voice was low and melodious and as beautiful as was she. But as the single, musical word resonated inside the young man's head, it was met there by a strange, gray static. He was suddenly dizzy; the floor rocked precariously beneath his feet, and he was forced to grip the wall for support.

"You look weak. Come and sit down," the woman invited, and patted the pristine bed sheets with one milky hand. Her long, painted fingernails stood out like ripe berries against a snowy backdrop.

The young man produced a handkerchief from one of his pockets and began to wipe his suddenly moist brow.

"I'm sorry," he said. "I believe I'm alright, but for a moment...I suspect it's just the heat. It's very crowded in here," he explained.

The woman smiled more broadly, displaying a perfect, white row of small, even teeth.

"It is crowded out *there*," she said, gesturing slightly toward the door. "In here it is very intimate, don't you think?"

The young man could only nod. The party, with its oppressive noise and its collection of hot, animated bodies, did seem very far away. By contrast, the small bedroom was hushed and cool.

Strange, then, that I am perspiring so, the young man thought, and passed his handkerchief once more across his brow.

"Sit."

It was less an invitation than a command. The young man responded obediently, crossing the floor and taking a seat on the edge of the bed, next to the chair.

He had never been so close to her before. It was intoxicating.

Her skin appeared poreless, as fine and pale as bone china. Her eyes were large, dark mirrors. It was her scent, though—the heavy, dark fragrance of dried flowers—that caused the young man to have to steady himself again. He had had beautiful women in the past; he was good-looking himself and in a profession that attracted the fairer sex, but he had never before been so sensually overwhelmed in the presence of a woman.

He felt a powerful urge to surrender to the sensations that were sweeping over him. He imagined laying himself open, becoming willing to drink in her gorgeous perfection and honestly share every indecent thought and wild emotion that ran through him. Instead, the part of him that had been steeped in propriety took over, and he asked her:

"The apartment—is it yours, then?"

The woman appeared amused by the attempt at conversation.

"It is Rena's," she said.

Without asking, the young man knew that Rena was the short woman with the frizzy black halo of ringlets.

"It is ours to use, however," the woman continued, and she leaned suggestively toward the young man. Her breath was an icy breeze upon his face, and he felt his heart begin to pound.

"I saw you earlier," he gasped, "at the reception. I wanted so much to meet you."

The woman's lips were only inches from his own.

"And I have been waiting to meet you," she said.

"Then we are both...attracted..." he whispered. "Both willing..." The words took all of the young man's strength. The buzzing had returned to his head, and dark blotches interrupted his vision. The woman smiled at him—winningly, he was sure—but in his sickened state, he saw a certain grotesqueness to it, something writhing and dark beneath the flawless, blonde facade. Her teeth, which he knew were perfect pearls, now appeared to have razor-sharp points.

I am hallucinating, he thought. *I am fevered.*

The woman reached to caress the young man, and with his last strength, he pushed her away.

"I'm sorry," he panted. "So very sorry. But I believe I am ill, and I don't want to ruin what could be quite wonderful." With Herculean effort, he rose to his feet. His legs felt like jelly, but he made them carry him back to the bedroom door.

The young man turned to take one final look at what he was leaving. The woman had draped herself seductively across the bed. The evening gown had risen quite high upon her shapely thigh.

I am leaving that, he thought, and the thought pained him nearly as much as the sudden malady that held him in its grip.

"Please tell me that we will meet again," he pleaded.

The woman smiled. She raised her chin in a regal fashion and responded in her beautiful dulcet voice.

"I promise that we will," she said.

The young man was simultaneously filled with joy and revulsion. His illness, whatever it was, had him imagining that the stench of rotting garbage had infused the room. He began to gag. Before the gags could become retches, he opened the door and delivered himself out into the din of the party.

The room was no less congested than it had been before, and the air was no less choked with cigarette smoke and body odor. Still, as the young man pushed his way through the sweaty crowd, his head began to clear. By the time he had reached the other side of the room, he felt curiously well, as though he had never been sick at all.

He paused for a moment and wondered if it was not too late to go back. He could say something clever, like, "My darling, I was temporarily weakened by your overwhelming beauty." It would not even be much of a lie. The young man turned around and looked for the door that led to the bedroom where the beautiful woman lay on immaculate white sheets, waiting to seduce him.

He could see no door.

Leaning casually against the wall, in the place where he was quite certain he had exited, was the dark woman, Rena. She seemed to feel the young man's eyes upon her and turned to meet his gaze. When she saw his expression of utter confusion, her mouth twisted into a sneering laugh.

The young man turned quickly away.

I am not at all well, he thought. *Not at all.*

Comforting himself with the beautiful woman's promise that they would meet again, he let himself out into the hall.

As he turned into the stairwell, with its ugly plaster walls cast in deep shadows, something odd occurred to him.

He had just fallen deeply in love and did not even know the woman's name.

"Who was that?"

The girl, one of several pretty, fresh-faced ingenues at the party, had been watching as the young man hurriedly left the flat. She was struck by his dark, good looks.

The fellow who had been attempting to win the girl over with his witty conversation made every effort to appear less impressed.

"Oh, that's just Bela Blasko," he said in a weary, dismissive tone. "He fancies himself a bit of an actor. Sometimes calls himself Bela Lugosi..."

And then the fellow returned to his impressive stories of the theater, and the girl turned her attention back to him, and, for the time being, all was well.

Bela Lugosi

Bela Lugosi eventually left Hungary for America, where he was destined to become a star of the stage and screen. He was best known for his portrayal of Dracula, a role he originated on Broadway and later made famous in the movies.

In 1955, Lugosi was interviewed on NBC Radio and spoke at length about some of the seemingly supernatural incidents that had taken place in his own life. One of the stories he shared was the tale of his strange infatuation with a beautiful young woman he had known in Hungary. Each time they met, he felt physically exhausted, dizzy and ill—still, he could not resist her charms. Lugosi said that only by traveling across the ocean to a new land did he manage to break the spell that the woman held over him.

Her skin, he said, was extremely pale, and she had sharply pointed teeth...

In 1956, Bela Lugosi died. According to his final request, he was buried in his Count Dracula costume, complete with satin-lined cape.

Perfect Rose

What happened that day, in Daniel Chen's office, had happened many times before. A great many times, in fact, so it was not shock that forced his decision so much as weariness.

He had been in a long, tiresome meeting with a buyer who had just placed a large order for an assortment of ornamental goods that Daniel imported. As the two men concluded their business, they rose to shake hands. That was when the buyer, a youngish, expensively dressed fellow named Watkins, noticed the photograph.

"Beautiful!" he said, and picked the picture up by its tasteful pewter frame. He gazed admiringly for a moment or two, then, with a raised eyebrow, asked Daniel, "Your daughter?"

Daniel took the photo out of the other man's hands and returned it to its precise angle on the massive rosewood desktop.

"My wife," he said, somewhat abruptly.

"Well," said Watkins, the buyer, and it was obvious that he was searching for an appropriate comment.

"Well, good for you. She's a knockout," was what he settled on.

An hour after the fellow had left, Daniel Chen sat in his butter-soft leather chair, staring out his broad office window at the blue expanse that was San Francisco Bay. In his hands, he held the photograph of his wife. The glass front was marked with his fingerprints, which did nothing to obscure the beauty of her image. She was lovely, and she did look young, and Daniel knew that he could not blame people for assuming that he was a rich old man with a trophy wife.

It's just that he *wasn't*. And he hated to have others think it.

It made him look shallow; it made him seem common, and he had strived for all of his life to be neither. The problem was that, while he had been striving, his body had grown old. He was a 62-year-old man with a thick waist, a lined face, drooping eyelids and yellowing teeth. That would have been acceptable had he married a woman who had aged with him—graying, stooping, becoming more plump and less vivacious as time marched on. But he had not married such a woman; he had married Rose, and Rose seemed to be defying the very laws of nature.

Rose looked as beautiful, and appeared to be as young, as the day they had first met.

Daniel had been a student then—learning the art of business as he prepared to assume the reins of his father's small store. He had told his parents that Rose was also a student. In fact, she was a drifter who worked as a waitress or a laundress whenever she lit someplace for more than a few days. Daniel didn't care. When he looked at her, his heart ached, and he knew that he would never again feel complete on his own.

When they had known each other for only 10 days, he proposed.

"I love you," he had dared to tell her in the middle of dim sum, "and although I don't have much to offer now, I promise to work very hard. If your parents will agree, I want to marry you."

"Daniel," she had replied softly, and smiled, as though he had said something quite silly and endearing. "My parents have been dead for very many years. I can speak for myself and, yes, I happily accept."

They had kissed then, in the middle of the restaurant, in front of their plates of pork buns and sticky rice. It was a moment of pure joy. When it ended, Rose looked at Daniel with an intensity that he had never known a woman to show.

"I promise you that I will make a good wife," she said. And then, she did.

For many years, Daniel Chen could find no fault with his wife. She was kind to him and loving, and she quietly supported everything that he did. There were no children, but in his heart, Daniel did not want any, so he never complained. Rose was all he ever needed. With her at his side, he built his business into something his father could never have dreamed of and led a happy life.

Rose's singular beauty definitely contributed to his happiness. She had translucent skin and glossy black hair and unusual jade green eyes that tilted at a perfect angle. Daniel was a proud man when he had Rose on his arm. Then, when they had been married for 30 years, that changed.

On their 10th anniversary, Daniel had patted his own expanding waistline and complimented his wife for keeping so trim. When they celebrated 20 years of wedded bliss, he had compared his graying temples to Rose's ebony mane and had been silently pleased that she took such meticulous care of herself. On the 30th anniversary of their marriage, however, Daniel found that he was reluctant to take his usual stock of Rose's appearance. The occasion forced him to realize that his lovely wife was 50 years of age and was looking as fresh and vital as she had when she was 20.

There were no creases around her eyes; there was no slackness in her skin. She had never suffered a day of illness or fatigue. Her vision, hearing and reflexes were those of a young girl, and she was as energetic as one who was in the prime of life. Daniel searched for an answer and, for a time, tried to congratulate himself for Rose's preservation.

You've given her a happy life, he told himself. *What worries has she had to line her face?* It was an explanation that did not ring true, however, and as time went on, Daniel's discomfort grew.

Daniel felt more acutely aware of his own deterioration when Rose showed none. He worried that he appeared foolish in her presence, like an old man who was using his wealth to buy affection. And then there was the thing that he could barely permit himself to think about. It was a legend; it was nonsense; Daniel berated himself constantly for being superstitious. Eventually, however, he could not stop himself from wanting to find out if it was true.

The day after the buyer named Watkins left his office in embarrassment, Daniel Chen sought the advice of an expert.

She was an ancient woman, a psychic from the old country, who occupied a filthy suite of rooms above a small grocery in the heart of Chinatown.

"You want to know something about your wife," she croaked before Daniel had even taken a seat. He nodded, numbly.

"She does not age," he confessed to the hag. "She has not aged a day in several decades."

The psychic nodded knowingly.

"So, you are wondering if she is one of the cursed ones."

Daniel Chen did not answer directly, and he stared at his hands as he spoke.

"My grandmother used to tell me stories, when I was a boy," he said. "I never believed them. I thought they were legends, superstitions. But now, I am unsure. Now, I am desperate to know."

"The vampires never grow old," confirmed the psychic, with a nod. "But there is only one way to know for certain if your wife suffers from this curse. You must keep her from going out at night. She must be confined. Perhaps there's a hospital, where she could be held for observation." She spoke the last word slowly, weighting it with innuendo.

"Will I be certain?" Daniel wanted to know.

"Quite certain, quite certain," the old woman sang, and she began to rock to and fro in a manner that told Daniel she had exhausted her allotment of lucidity for the day. He put two $50 bills on the tattered silk embroidery that covered the table and left.

Several days later, Daniel Chen sat his wife down on their expensive brocade sofa and gently explained that he had committed her to an asylum.

"I don't understand," Rose said to him, again and again.

"It is for your health," was all the explanation Daniel offered.

"But my health is fine," Rose protested. "I feel perfectly well, Daniel. And I think," she lowered her voice judiciously, as there were already two large orderlies waiting in the foyer to take her away, "I think there is something you are not telling me."

"It's much like a spa, and it's only for a month, Rose," is all that Daniel would say. Then he kissed his wife on the cheek and looked away as she was whisked off to the luxurious clinic, which had been carefully chosen for its discretion and its reputation for dealing with strange and rare disorders.

Several days passed, during which Rose railed against her imprisonment. Many times each day, she would phone her husband to complain bitterly about her predicament and beg for release. Eventually, Daniel requested that her telephone privileges be revoked. At the end of the first week, however, he received another call from the clinic. That time, it was not Rose. It was her doctor.

"Your wife suffered a psychotic episode last evening," he said. "I think that we should discuss it."

The doctor told Daniel that Rose had managed to slip out of her room and past the duty nurse on the previous night. An alarm had been raised immediately, but it still took more than an hour to locate the missing woman. When they found her, it was in the closet-like room that served as the clinic's small blood bank. Rose was sitting on the cold, tile floor, with empty plastic containers littered around her. Her lips, her chin and the front of her white hospital gown were smeared bright red. She had been gorging on blood.

"We took an inventory," said the doctor. "There were more than six pints missing. It's quite interesting, actually. She claims she needs it to live."

At the other end of the line, there was silence. Daniel Chen was holding the phone in one hand and his pounding head in the other. Finally, he spoke.

"Guard her more carefully," he instructed. "Do what you have to do."

An orderly was assigned to watch Rose Chen at all times. Restraints were kept upon her, even while she slept. After a while, she stopped begging for her freedom, a sign that the doctor took to be positive.

"You are accepting your fate," he explained to her, "and that is the first step toward recovery."

Rose said nothing. She appeared to be lacking the energy for argument. In the days that she had spent in the clinic, her jade green eyes had grown dull and lifeless, and dark shadows had bloomed beneath them. Her hair had lost some of its luster, and her complexion had become sallow. She looked weak and lethargic and appeared quite harmless. It was for this reason that the nurse felt no concern when, on the 15th day of her stay, Rose requested that her wristbands be loosened.

"Please," she whispered, and her voice was as dry and as thin as a piece of tissue. "These straps are so tight, and my wrists have been rubbed raw."

Rose looked so pathetic, so small and shriveled in her hospital bed, that the nurse took pity.

"I can loosen them a little, Mrs. Chen," she said, in a soothing tone. Then she smiled and whispered conspiratorially, "But it must be our secret."

A moment later, the nurse was screaming for the orderly, for the doctor, for anyone and everyone, to come to her aid. She had lost all interest in keeping things secret.

"She tried to kill me!" the nurse wailed several minutes later when the doctor finally joined the small crowd that had gathered in Rose Chen's tastefully appointed private room. "I leaned over her, and she attacked me viciously! Look!" The nurse pulled back the blood-soaked cloth that she had been holding to the side of her neck, revealing the savage bite marks that were there. The doctor nodded absentmindedly and favored the nurse with a glance, but it was Rose who held captive his attention.

She was strapped to the rails of her bed with a number of broad leather bands. The restraints held her securely, despite the way she was writhing and straining against them. Rose's head was not held down, and it thrashed from side to side, whipping her mass of brittle, tangled hair across her face.

When her hair flipped back for a moment, the doctor could see that Rose Chen had her mouth forced open to an impossibly huge angle. Her lower jaw appeared nearly unhinged, the gap was so large. Over her bottom lip, which had been stretched taut and white, her tongue darted frantically.

The doctor realized that she was trying desperately to lick up the last, unreachable drops of the nurse's blood that painted her chin and cheeks.

He had to turn away immediately to stop himself from vomiting. Then the doctor walked quickly out of the room and went looking for the administrator.

"Get her husband down here," was all he said.

Daniel arrived at the hospital the next afternoon. He was early for his appointment with the doctor and decided that he would first look in on his wife. He walked into what he thought was Rose's room and saw a pale, old woman sleeping there. He had turned and begun to tiptoe out, thinking that he would locate a nurse who could tell him where to find Rose, when she spoke to him.

"Daniel," she said, in a warbling voice that he did not recognize. "You've finally come for me!"

Daniel Chen turned and looked at the crone who lay in his wife's bed and was repulsed to see that she was gazing at him with obsessive affection. Her puckered mouth drew back into a parched smile.

"Come sit with me," she said.

Daniel did not move from his position near the door.

"I have to find my wife," he explained and reached for the door handle.

"Stop!" the old woman shrieked at Daniel, startling him so that he pulled his hand back.

"I am your wife," she spat, "and you have to help me! Please. Daniel, please."

Daniel looked at the hag, at the outline of her wrinkled face and the set of her mouth. She stared back at him with eyes that were beginning to dull with cataracts. Beneath the filmy veil, the irises still appeared to be a most unusual shade of green.

"Rose?" Daniel said, and his voice was thick with tears. "How could this have happened?"

"Free me, Daniel," Rose begged. "I am so weak and hungry. Please don't let me die, here, please."

Daniel was overwhelmed with pity and remorse and went to the bedside to comfort his wife. He stroked her coarse, white hair and held her thin hand.

"What can I do, Rose?" he finally asked.

"Remove the restraints," she pleaded. "Take me home."

"And will you get well again?" he asked, hopefully.

"I will go on," she whispered. "I can go on forever, as I am."

Daniel fingered the thick leather straps and metal buckles that fastened his wife to her deathbed. He began to undo one, then stopped and patted Rose's shoulder.

"If you are to get well," he said, "you must stay in hospital. It is for your own good, Rose." He turned then, and without looking back, walked away.

"Daniel!" Rose called after him, and there was panic in her voice. "Daniel!"

Before the hydraulic door could close behind him, Daniel was forced to hear Rose's final comment.

"I was always a good wife to you," she cried.

When Rose Chen finally died, on her 20th day at the clinic, she appeared to be much older than her supposed 60 years. The doctors and nurses were mystified, but agreed that the merciful thing had happened.

"She suffered terribly, with that ailment," one of them said.

At the funeral, all of the mourners whispered in agreement that Daniel looked devastated. He did, and he was, for he had truly loved his beautiful Rose.

Afterwards, he was occasionally bothered by ugly doubts about whether he had done the right thing. He always comforted himself in the same way, with the knowledge that he had really had no choice.

After all, he told himself, how would it have looked? A successful, vibrant man like Daniel Chen, with such an old wife.

In his book Strange Monsters and Madmen *(Popular Library, 1969), Warren Smith wrote of a similar case involving one of the legendary ageless vampires of Asia. In the story, Smith put forth two theories—one scientific and one supernatural—to explain the phenomenon.*

Smith quoted a doctor named Chiang as saying, "The psychiatric textbooks contain some information on these rare instances where a patient becomes totally convinced of the necessity for blood as a sustenance to remain alive."

Then there was the opinion of an unnamed professor who stated that "Chinese history has always included tales of vampire women...They must drink blood to remain young forever."

It is impossible to say whether such women—if, indeed, they do exist—are the victims of an occult curse or a rare psychiatric disorder.

The mystery will likely never be solved.

Nasty

Robbie had seen kids like that before—kids with dirty faces and shabby clothes and unkempt hair and black lines of crud beneath the edges of their fingernails. He had seen them, and he knew that his Grandma Lil had a name for them: she called them nasty.

There were nasty children everywhere, according to Robbie's grandmother. Sometimes they were at the grocery store, looking hungry and thin as rails and ready to steal something if they didn't get a handout. There was a boy who would trim anybody's lawn for five bucks, and Grandma Lil said that he was nasty, what with his permanently downcast gaze and permanently grass-stained knees. And the brother and sister who lived in the trailer next to Robbie and his grandmother—nasty without a doubt. They were pale and dull looking, with wide-set, vacant eyes and a penchant for using dirty words. Their mother had smoked marijuana when she was pregnant with them, Lil once confided to Robbie, so you know they couldn't help turning out the way that they did. Nasty.

Robbie wasn't peering over the dry, split boards of his grandmother's fence at the neighbor kids, though. He was in his daddy's pickup truck, drinking an Orange Crush and reading a comic book by the glowing neon sign of a Tex-Mex roadhouse called Rosa's. The kids—two grubby, skinny boys with bare feet—were on the other side of the big, dirt parking lot, hanging around a 50-gallon drum that had been painted with the word "trash."

They were making Robbie a little nervous. Every time

he glanced up from his comic, they seemed to be looking at him or were just looking away. He figured that the one was littler than he was and that he might even outweigh the tall one. But there were two of them, and sometimes nasty kids liked to gang up on kids like him, just out of pure envy. So he kept the doors of the truck locked, and he kept the windows rolled up, despite the August Texas heat, and he reminded himself that his daddy would run out of money after four beers—five at the most—and then he would come out and drive them both home. Lil always told Robbie not to let his father drive if he'd had more than three drinks. Robbie felt it was pointless to tell her that when a guy was nine years old, the amount of control he had over such situations was nil. Why get her upset, he figured. She didn't have control over most situations herself.

Robbie tilted the pop bottle straight up, to drain out the very last drops. As his head tipped back, he noticed the two kids kicking gravel at each other, by the trash barrel. When his head came back down, he saw that they were gone. His eyes strained to see better in the neon-lit night, to see if there were any bare feet and scrawny limbs behind the vehicles on that dark side of the lot. He couldn't see any movement, though, and decided that the boys must have taken off across the highway.

"Hey, kid."

Robbie's heart leaped. His body followed, and the empty Orange Crush bottle hit the floorboards with a dull *thud*. He turned, wild-eyed, in the direction of the voice and saw that the two kids were standing by the driver's side window.

They looked older than Robbie had imagined. Not bigger, but older. The taller of the two, especially, wore an expression of calm confidence that Robbie usually associated with authority figures. It was a look that belonged on his principal, Mr. Cook, or the guy with the Cadillac who came on the first Monday of every month to collect his grandmother's rent check. It didn't belong on a barefoot kid who looked like he hadn't had a meal all week.

"What's up, kid? Whatcha doing here?"

The boy offered Robbie a cold little smile. It didn't have a drop of friendliness in it.

"I'm just waiting," Robbie said. There was a pause, and he decided that it would be prudent to add, "My dad's gonna be out in a minute."

The younger boy looked up at his friend. He said nothing, but there was worry written in his features. The older kid stayed cool. If there was a problem, he wasn't letting on.

"A minute, huh?" he said. "Well, that's okay. We only need a minute. Can you let us in the truck?"

The request sounded so matter-of-fact, so *reasonable*, that Robbie actually reached for the door lock. Then he stopped himself and looked up in time to see something like anger flash across the older kid's face. It took only a second for the boy's features to become smooth and bland again, though. He raised an eyebrow at Robbie then, as if to say *problem?*

"What do you want to come in the truck for?" asked Robbie.

"We want to show you something," said the boy. "Something cool. Open up."

"I can see from here."

The older boy started to laugh, then, and he shook his head as though he was dealing with the world's biggest baby.

"No, kid, you don't get it. Don't you want to be cool? If you open the door, I'll show you something that you've never seen before. Just open the door."

As if on cue, the front door to Rosa's opened then, and three men in denim jackets and gimme caps walked out. A slice of yellow light and Emmylou Harris bluegrass spilled into the parking lot with them. Robbie looked and saw that none of the men was his father. The disappointment on his face was easy to read.

"Guess your daddy's not coming for a while yet, kid. I bet someone in there is buying him rounds of beers. You might be out here for a long time." The boy pressed his face right up against the window then and said, "Let us in, and we'll wait together. There's nothing to be afraid of. We're just kids, like you."

Suddenly, Robbie felt overwhelmingly lonely. Between the kids that Grandma Lil told him he was too good to play with and the kids that he never met while he waited outside bars for his alcoholic father, Robbie didn't have much company.

These guys didn't seem bad. Deep down, he wasn't a snob; he didn't care if they were dressed like charity cases. And he didn't care if they got some dirt on the upholstered bench seat of his old man's truck. He felt like hanging out with someone, and he reached over to pull up the little button that kept the door locked.

Then the door to Rosa's opened up again, and Robbie's daddy came skidding out on his back. A big guy with a muscle shirt and a black handlebar moustache threw his hat out after him.

"Get lost, deadbeat!" the big guy yelled, and Robbie knew that his father had, once again, been ordering beers after he ran out of money. He felt ashamed and turned to see what his new friends thought.

Their faces were etched with desperation.

"Hurry!" the older kid begged. "Hurry, he's coming. Let us in the truck, now!"

The little kid remained mute, but pawed at the glass with grimy fingers. Robbie gaped at them, bewildered, and it was then that he noticed their eyes.

They were like bottomless, black lakes.

They weren't brown; they weren't gray; they were the color of jet, with no distinction between the pupil and the iris.

"Let us *in! Let us in!*"

Robbie was still staring at those bizarre, coal-black orbs when, suddenly, the two boys vanished. Where they had been standing, pleading with him, his father now stood, fumbling with his keys.

"For chrissake, Robbie, are you gonna open the door, or make me stand here in the dark looking for the damn key?"

Robbie blinked, then spun himself 360 degrees, looking for the kids. He couldn't see them. He wasn't exactly sure how that made him feel.

He reached over and popped the lock for his daddy, who opened the door and grunted as he slid in behind the wheel. He smelled like beer and cigarettes. The only time that ever changed was first thing in the morning, when he smelled like coffee and cigarettes.

Robbie's father turned to look at him and gave a snort of laughter.

"You're sweatin' like a pig, boy," he said. "I don't know why you didn't roll down the windows."

Then he started the pickup's motor and slowly weaved out of the parking lot and up onto the highway.

All the way into Abilene, father and son didn't share a word. It was their usual rapport, and, for once, Robbie was glad of it. It gave him time to calm down without having to make conversation.

Finally, when the city lights began to roll moving patterns across the truck's shiny engine hood, Robbie's daddy found something to say.

"I'm gonna hit a few more places tonight," he said. "You want to go back to Lil's?"

"Sure." Robbie felt relief. He wouldn't have to deal with his father's hangover, come morning. More important, he wouldn't have to spend any more time that night waiting around while his daddy ordered beers he couldn't pay for and scary, black-eyed kids tried to talk their way into the truck.

Robbie was actually starting to relax, when there was a tapping on the glass directly behind his head. He glanced sideways at his daddy, who gave no indication of having heard anything. Of course, he was applying all of his half-lidded concentration on keeping the truck between the lines.

Tap-tap-tap.

Robbie turned, slowly. He saw what he feared he would see.

There they were, the nasty kids from the parking lot. They were in the box of the truck, just inches away from Robbie, with nothing separating them but a pane of GM glass. They were smiling, and the bigger kid was saying something. Between the road noise and the engine, Robbie couldn't hear him, but he could read lips well enough.

"Let us in," he was saying. *"You have to let us in."*

Robbie turned back toward the windshield and decided that he would stay facing forward unless he heard glass starting to break behind his head.

When his father left him in the dim circle of Grandma Lil's porch light, the two boys were nowhere to be seen. But that night, while Robbie lay in his little single bed under the quilt that smelled like stale laundry, he couldn't sleep, because of the scratching sounds at his window...

It was nearly dawn when Robbie lost consciousness, so he didn't get out of bed until almost noon. Grandma Lil was less than pleased.

"Lazy, like your father," she pronounced as she sat at the kitchen table, smoking a cigarette. "Good thing I wasn't depending on you for anything this morning."

"I'm sorry," mumbled Robbie, over his cereal. "I had trouble sleeping."

"You slept well enough while I was working to fix up the damage that your daddy did last night."

"What damage?" Robbie's head was fuzzy and throbbing. He was wondering if someone could get a hangover by association.

"What damage!" Lil's voice was laced with disgust, and she stabbed the butt of her cigarette into the little ceramic ashtray that she carried around the trailer, like a change purse. "When that drunken idiot drove up, he knocked over two of my little Bambis and the gnome that sits on my geranium planter!" There was fury twisting Lil's heavily made-up face. She thought of herself as a gardener and considered her fading, plastic lawn ornaments to be things of beauty.

Robbie sighed.

"I'm sorry, Grandma Lil," he said. "Sorry you had to fix it by yourself."

"Save your concern, buster. I had help. There are some kids in this neighborhood that don't spend the entire damn morning in bed."

"Who helped you?" Robbie asked. He was genuinely curious. His grandmother was an unpopular woman in the trailer park, amongst both the grownups and the kids.

"I don't know their names," Grandma Lil said. "It was a couple of boys, real polite kids, even if they did look all dirty and nasty. They were out there this morning trying to set my garden back up, even before I got to it."

Robbie had stopped eating. He had lost his appetite.

"So what happened, Grandma Lil? Where did they go?" Robbie kept his voice calm, but his pulse had begun to pound in his ears.

"Well, how the hell should I know?" Lil screeched at him. "Do I look like the county warden?" Then she lit another cigarette, took a long drag and calmed down. "I can tell you where they'll be tonight, though," she said.

"Where?" asked Robbie, dully, although he already knew the answer.

"Right here," said Lil, jabbing her finger at the table, for emphasis. "I figured, kids like that, they need a home-cooked meal more than they need pocket change. So I told 'em to come back tonight, and I'll fry some hamburgers. They looked real pleased, Robbie. Real happy to get the invitation."

"I bet they were," Robbie said, and his voice felt faraway. Inside his head, there was another voice—a desperate, panicked, pleading voice.

Let us in! it shrieked. *Let us in!*

And now, thought Robbie, with growing terror, *now they have an invitation.*

He had seen enough movies and read enough horror comics to know that Grandma Lil's hamburgers were going to go to waste.

Because, if Robbie wasn't mistaken, things were about to get nasty.

In the last few years, a number of disturbingly similar stories have been posted on the Internet. They all share certain common elements: children—usually two, or three—with strange, black eyes, who try to convince someone to admit them to their vehicle or house. The people who are approached are usually filled with dread but still feel compelled to do as the children say.

Tradition tells us that vampires cannot enter a person's home until they have been invited. Are these children modern-day vampires, or is this simply an urban legend that is borrowing from the popular lore? It's impossible to say.

Still, it's always wise to be cautious when dealing with strangers, no matter how young and harmless they may appear to be.

Part Four

Ghosts

Everyone loves a good ghost story. And in recent years, more and more people are out to prove that these tales can be as easily rooted in fact as in fiction. There is a tremendously heightened interest in true ghost lore, as is evidenced by the variety of non-fiction books, documentary-style television shows and the growing numbers of associations devoted to hunting and studying these elusive phantoms.

Conclusive proof has yet to be found, but as data accumulate, categories are emerging regarding different types of hauntings. Exceptions exist for every rule—particularly in an area as open to interpretation as is this one—but it would seem that most ghosts fall into one of three classifications.

There are spirits who are apparently intelligent and aware. They react to the circumstances and people around them. There are other ghosts classified as "residual hauntings." They are less agents than imprints that have been left upon their surroundings. And then there are the specters who continue *about the business of their lives simply because they have not yet realized that they are dead—a situation that seems to occur when death is sudden and unexpected. These phantoms become frustrated when they can't negotiate the physical landscape with their accustomed ease and are understandably upset when other people move into their homes, jobs and even marriages.*

Categories aside, what all ghosts have in common is enduring dramatic appeal. When we wish to be entertained, there is nothing quite as appealing as a tale of something that goes bump in the night...

The April Ghost

"She was wearing a suit, a sort of brown—suit-thing. The jacket was kind of—I don't know—fitted at the waist, you know what I mean? There were buttons down the front. It was very old-fashioned looking. It was brown. Oh, right, I said that."

Martin shook his head and reached for his glass of wine. He considered himself to be well spoken on many topics, but found his vocabulary frustratingly limited when it came to describing women's clothing. He knew what he had seen, though. Of that, he was certain.

As was Bill.

"Like I always say, 'When you're right, you're right, and when you're wrong, you're Martin,'" he quipped. "But you know, buddy, you're even more wrong today than usual. How you could mistake a white wedding dress for a brown suit is entirely—I mean, *entirely*—beyond me."

Martin and Bill were brothers. The argument they were having was just the current variation of the same one they had been having since childhood. No matter what the issue was, Martin was always obsessed with convincing Bill that he was right. Bill, on the other hand, always held complete confidence in his own correctness and didn't care much whether Martin agreed with him or not. It was this casual arrogance that Martin considered to be so infuriating.

"How can you *say* that?!" he said, in a voice that was just a bit too loud for the dark, intimate bistro in which they were dining. "I mean, how do you just...you're just..."

"Food's here." Martin's wife, Jackie, a brunette mouse who had grown so accustomed to the arguments that she rarely bothered to pay attention to the details, interrupted her husband in mid-sputter.

The elderly waiter—the sort who could never get work at one of the popular chain restaurants but was just right for the kind of candle-in-a-bottle establishment that they were in that night—placed three huge plates of pasta on the table. He dusted each one with ground pepper and put a bowl of freshly grated Parmesan in the middle of the table.

"Enjoy," he said, in his cultured old-man voice, and then he was gone.

Bill looked enthusiastic about his food.

"Fabulous!" he said. "Look at this, Marty, that's *fresh* pasta! Didn't I tell you this place was good? You know who told me about it? Do you remember that blonde girl who..."

"We're not changing the subject."

"What?" Bill stuffed a forkful of linguini into his mouth.

"We were talking about the ghost, and we're not going to talk about anything else until we *finish* talking about the ghost!" A creeping red warmth had begun to spread across Martin's neck and ears.

Bill remained entirely unflustered.

"Sorry, Martin. I didn't know it was that important to you." Bill turned to Jackie with a mocking expression. It wasn't sly, or secretive. He wanted Martin to see.

Jackie smiled a little, but behind her hand. She had to live with Martin, and his moods.

"I think you're both right," she said, diplomatically.

"That's ridiculous," said Martin.

"Why?" Jackie was refilling her wine glass. She usually required a minimum half bottle to tolerate an evening with Martin and Bill. "You know, we're not talking about an everyday occurrence, here. We saw a ghost. Who's to say that she can't appear in different ways to different people?"

"I don't know, Jack." Martin twirled his fork busily in his pasta. He didn't want to be philosophical. He wanted to be right. "It sounds farfetched, to me. If we saw her on different days, maybe, or under different circumstances—say daylight and darkness. But we all saw her tonight, and she was in a *brown suit.*" He delivered the last two words aggressively, in the direction of his brother.

"Wedding dress," Bill said mildly, and drained his glass. Then, with mock sincerity, he added, "Look, Mart-o, the important thing—the only thing that *really* matters—is that we need more wine." He signaled across the room to the waiter, who acknowledged him with a small nod.

Martin was hunched over his meal, pouting, when something occurred to him. He sat up very suddenly, an expression of revelation lighting his face.

"Wait a minute—this is easy to solve," he said.

Bill and Jackie stole glances at one another, then both looked at Martin expectantly.

"Jackie, you saw her, too," Martin said. "So you're the deciding vote. Tell us—what was the ghost wearing?"

Jackie cleared her throat. Both Martin and Bill were staring at her. She was rarely the center of attention when the brothers were together, and it felt unfamiliar and uncomfortable.

"Well," she said, "a brown suit."

"*Aha!*" Martin jabbed his finger in Bill's face.

"And a wedding dress."

"A-ha-*ha*-ha!" retorted Bill.

"That's not funny." The pout settled back on Martin's face. "You should be helping us figure this out," he said. *You should be backing up my story*, he meant.

"Look, I'm just telling you what I saw." Jackie put down her fork and leaned back with a sigh.

"Martin—remember when we first got to the golf course, and we were walking along that path, on the way to meet Bill?"

Martin nodded and grunted around a mouthful of food.

"Okay," Jackie said. "Well, there was a woman who passed us on the path. She looked—I don't know exactly how to describe it—*distraught*, in some way. And after she walked by, I felt horrible. Just filled with dread. I would have just turned around and gone home at that point, but we'd planned to meet Bill."

"Hey, thanks for not standing me up, baby," Bill winked.

The waiter arrived at the table with another bottle of wine, which he expertly uncorked. When he walked away, Martin picked up the conversation.

"I don't remember meeting *anyone* on the path," he said.

"I don't think you did," Jackie agreed. "I've been mulling it over ever since, and I think I was the only one who saw her there. *And*," Jackie gestured with her fork for emphasis, "she was wearing a brown suit."

"How did you know she was a ghost?" Bill asked.

"I didn't know at the time. I just knew that she had passed on a very bad vibe." As soon as Jackie finished speaking, she cast a nervous look at Martin. He hated for her to use what he called "hippie psychology." True to form, he winced at the word "vibe."

Jackie took a deep breath and continued.

"But when we were out on the green later, when I saw her the second time, I recognized her face. But this time she was wearing a wedding dress. That's when I was with Bill, and you had just...gone back to the car."

Jackie phrased it delicately, but all three of them knew that Martin had actually thrown a tantrum about some small thing and stormed off on his own.

"Um," Martin said and stroked his goatee. It was a nervous habit that cropped up whenever he was trying to hide embarrassment. "Well, it just seemed that we weren't having any luck together, and I thought I'd try a little ghost hunting off on my own. And, you know, it worked. Because that's when I saw her, when I was alone. She looked almost ordinary until I realized that she wasn't really walking. She was kind of—*skimming* over the ground. And then, a few seconds later, you guys came running up, saying you'd just seen the ghost."

"Yeah, that was a *Twilight Zone* moment, eh, Jacks?" Bill shook his head in wonder, and Jackie nodded in agreement.

"Yeah," she said, "it was something," and the tiniest of smiles played on her lips.

Bill, who generally never had an unexpressed thought, was wearing the same secretive, pleased expression. Martin looked from one to the other. His earlobes began to redden.

"So—do you think that she was in two places at one time? Was that it?" he asked. His eyes had grown narrow.

"I don't follow you." Bill had already emptied his plate, pushed it off to the side and was perusing the dessert menu. "Tiramisu, Marty. Check it out." He turned the small, leather-bound booklet and pointed to the item for all to see. "I'm having tiramisu," he declared.

Martin was showing no interest in dessert.

"What I mean is, I saw the ghost in one place, at a certain time. And then, I'd have to say almost immediately, you two showed up saying that you, also, had *just* seen the ghost. So—I don't get that. Do you think that she was able to be two places at once, and with different wardrobes at that?"

"I dunno. Maybe. What do you think, Jackie?" Bill was deeply involved in the dessert menu again. When he did look up from it on occasion, it was to scan the dark little restaurant, in search of their waiter.

"I don't know," Jackie said. Her eyes had become fixed upon her plate, and she began to busily push noodles around in the pools of sauce that had gathered there. "Is it important?"

"It might be," said Martin, and his voice was like silk.

"Garçon! Excellent..." Bill managed to catch the waiter's attention.

"Here's what I consider to be the problem—logistically speaking, that is," Martin continued. "You said that you saw the ghost right after I—left—and that would be a good half hour before I saw her. Another way to put it would be to say that you *saw* her a good half hour before you *said* you saw her."

Martin was glaring at Jackie.

"So I don't think we saw her at the same time, did we, Jackie? I think you and Bill saw her, floating around in her wedding dress, and then I think you *lost* about a half hour somewhere, which makes me wonder whether we *also* ran into some kind of bloody *time warp* this evening!"

"Hey, calm, Marty, calm!" Bill raised his hands in a peaceful gesture. Martin turned to him with a look of pure spite.

"I'm calm," he spat. "I'm just calmly asking where the hell you were, with my *wife*, for the 30 minutes between the time you saw the ghost and the time you came trotting up to tell me about it. Or, for that matter, whether you even *saw* the damn ghost because, if you didn't, that would really explain why you don't know what she was wearing!"

People at the nearest tables had begun to sneak discreet glances at the threesome. Jackie noticed and felt her face flush with embarrassment.

"For god's sake, Martin! Keep it down," she hissed. "We can talk about this later! It's been a really strange night, with all this ghost business..."

"Ah, you've been hunting the April Ghost, eh?" It was the waiter, who had arrived at the table in time to overhear Jackie's words.

"The who-what?" asked Bill.

"The April Ghost. Doris Gravlin, out there at the Oak Bay Golf Course. They call her that sometimes because she seems to show up most often in April."

"You know much about her?" Martin cocked his head and, for the first time that evening, actually looked the waiter in the eye.

"I know enough. Lots of people who prowl around the golf course looking for her, they stop here afterward, because we're so close." The man started to collect the empty plates from the table.

"Then maybe you can tell me something," Martin said. He was talking to the waiter, but his eyes traveled from Bill to Jackie. "What sort of outfit does she wear?"

"Brown suit," the man answered, without hesitation. "Old-fashioned kind, with a peplum jacket."

Martin's eyes were bright and hard. His hands, which rested on the tablecloth, were balled into tight fists. His lips pulled into a bitter, little smile.

"I thought so," he said, and he delivered the words very slowly. There was satisfaction in his tone, but there was something else, too. He glanced up at Jackie and Bill.

"When you're building an alibi," he said softly, "you need to do a little research."

There was a minute filled with nothing but awkwardness then. Normally, Bill would have been ordering desserts and coffees and dessert coffees, topped with whipped cream and shaved chocolate. Instead, he was as quiet as the other two, waiting for the elderly server to leave the table so that explanations and soothing assurances could be issued.

After a micro-eternity, the waiter began to walk away with his armload of messy plates and silverware. Three steps from the table, he stopped and turned back.

"I just recalled," he said, "that some people have seen Doris in a wedding dress."

Jackie nearly melted with relief.

"There, you see, Martin?" she said. "Now do you believe us?"

For a moment, Martin did appear to soften. He stroked his goatee and lowered his eyes. He might have begun to apologize had the waiter not spoken again as he walked away.

"Suppose I should say that she appears to some *couples* in a wedding dress. They say only lovers see her dressed that way."

The man was nearly through the kitchen door, too far from the table to be heard, when he finished his thought.

"Course it's supposed to mean the relationship is doomed..." he said and dumped the dishes in the bus tray.

A few minutes later, the table sat empty. The waiter collected the small tray that held the bill and for the life of him couldn't understand why there was no tip.

On September 22, 1936, in Oak Bay, British Columbia, a 30-year-old private nurse named Doris Gravlin was reported missing. Five days later, a caddy from the Oak Bay Golf Course was in the process of searching for a lost ball when he discovered the woman's battered body. Ever since, Doris has haunted the golf course, making most of her spectral appearances in the spring, thereby earning the nickname "The April Ghost."

Doris Gravlin's spirit materializes wearing either an old-fashioned brown suit or a flowing white wedding gown. According to the folklore, couples who see Doris rushing toward them—with her arms outstretched and her filmy dress billowing around her—are destined to never marry.

One can't blame Doris for taking a dim view of romance. She was murdered by her estranged husband.

Wife

Danny Pierce shuffled through the blanket of fallen leaves that covered the cemetery and looked for a good place to sit and eat his sandwiches. It didn't take him long to find one. There was a tombstone that was just the right size to make a comfortable backrest, set in a place where he could see the road but wouldn't be too bothered by what was going on out there.

What was going on, on the dirt road near the cemetery, was a social event. In the years before the Depression, Danny thought that those same people might have gone to the movies, or to dances. But, as it was, they were making a night out of parking by Tabor Cemetery and trying to catch a glimpse of its famous ghost light.

A horn honked in the distance, announcing that another carload of thrill seekers were about to join the party. Danny shook his head in dismay and eased himself down to the ground.

He very nearly sat in someone else's lap.

"Oh, excuse me! I'm sorry!" he blurted, as much out of surprise as politeness. It was dark, particularly in the deep shadows cast by the trees that surrounded the small grave-yard. Danny had not seen the woman who already occupied the perfect viewing seat.

"Don't apologize," she said, in a friendly tone. "There is plenty of room. But perhaps we could sit side by side, instead of stacked up like cord wood." She moved several inches to her right and brushed away a few twigs, clearing a place for Danny to sit.

He hesitated for a moment. He hadn't really wanted company. If he had, he would have been out on the road leaning against one of the faded Model Ts and passing a jug of moonshine. Still, the woman was soft-spoken and friendly, despite the fact that he had nearly crushed her in his clumsiness. All things considered, Danny thought that sitting down would be the mannerly thing to do.

"Thanks," he said, and made himself comfortable on the patch of ground next to the woman.

Danny pulled the waxed paper bundle that contained his supper from the front pocket of his denim overalls.

"Would you like a sandwich?" he asked the woman, although, in his hungry state, he hoped that she would say no. When she did decline, as politely as she had offered to share her seat, he felt selfish.

"Are you sure?" he urged her, out of guilt. "It's bacon, on fried bread. Made 'em myself, before I walked over here."

"Thank you, but I'm really not hungry," the woman smiled.

It was a pretty smile, and Danny was charmed. He wiped the bacon grease from his palm on his pants leg and extended his hand.

"I'm Danny Pierce," he said.

The woman touched his hand with hers. Her skin was icy cold. Danny wasn't surprised; the woman was poorly dressed for a fall evening, even the warm one that it was. Her simple black dress had sleeves that stopped at the elbow, and she hadn't bothered to put on a coat.

"I'm Tom Munson's wife," she responded.

It seemed an odd thing to say. At first, Danny wondered if it was the woman's way of telling him that although she was sitting next to him in the cemetery, after dark, she was quite unavailable. Then he thought that she had perhaps given her husband's name as a reference, and he wondered if he knew a Tom Munson. As he rolled the name around in his mind, it did sound familiar.

"Munson," Danny mused, aloud. "Do I know your husband?"

"I don't think so," said the woman, putting an end to Danny's theory.

A sudden burst of laughter drew their attention toward what was happening out on the road. Someone had told a joke and appeared to be in the process of telling another. A semi-circle of people had gathered around to listen while they shared bottles of lemonade and ate pieces of johnnycake.

"Look at them," Danny said, with disgust. "They think it's a picnic."

The woman looked at Danny with amusement, and he remembered his own package of sandwiches.

"Well," he said, reddening, "you know what I mean. They don't take it seriously. They all say that they're here to look for the ghost light, but how could anyone possibly see it in the middle of all—*that*." Danny waved his hand in the direction of the crowd.

"It's true; it would be very difficult," agreed the woman. "Especially with all the other lights."

"That's right! That's absolutely right!" said Danny, suddenly feeling that he had discovered a kindred spirit. There had been many nights when he had simply given up and walked home, because of the distracting spectacle of headlights and camera flashes and the glowing red pinpoints of cigarettes being smoked in the crowd.

Just then, as if on cue, a flashbulb popped in the distance. Noises of surprise and excitement erupted, followed almost immediately by embarrassed giggles.

"See?" said Danny.

"I do," said the woman.

"That's probably that reporter fella from the *Leader-Post*," he said. "That's one of the reasons it's getting so crowded. Every time they write about the ghost light in the papers, it seems another dozen people come out here to see it."

It was true. As Danny had walked past the long line of parked vehicles that evening, he had noticed several that looked to be from farther away than Esterhazy. One had had Manitoba license plates on it; then there had been the shiny Chevrolet sedan that Danny was pretty sure belonged to the newspaper man. It had shapely fenders and chrome hubcaps, and in the midst of the pickup trucks and mud-splattered local cars, it looked like "city."

"You've been coming longer than any of them," said the woman.

"Well, yeah. I'm interested in the ghost light. I want to see it, you know? I think that would be real special. So I come here all the time."

"I know," said the woman.

"It's not a party to me," Danny stressed.

"I know that, too," said the woman.

Suddenly, Danny became aware that he had been doing most of the talking. He turned to regard his quiet companion. She looked calm and comfortable, somehow at home, leaning against the smooth granite with her long, sturdy legs crossed at the ankles and her dress smoothed primly over her knees. Danny was curious about her.

"So, 'Tom Munson's wife,' " he teased her. "Have you been out here before, hunting this will o' the wisp?"

"I'm here all the time," she said, in her soothing voice.

"I haven't seen you," he said.

"You weren't looking for me," she explained. "You were looking for the light." She pointed out toward the road, the crowded, noisy strip of dirt that the glowing phantom orb was said to travel.

Danny looked at the woman, with her calm voice and her quiet manner, and he felt a true sense of camaraderie. She was so much more serious about the light, so much more *reverent*, than the boisterous group on the road. He knew that he could ask her.

"Do you think..." he started, hesitantly. "Do you think that the light is the soul of someone who is buried here?" he asked. "Do you think that if we were to see that light, well, would it be proof, do you think, that our spirits go on?"

"I know that they do," the woman said. After a moment, she added, "What makes you so eager to know?"

"Well," Danny was staring at his hands, then busily re-wrapping the waxed paper around his last sandwich in precise folds. "I guess everybody's curious, right?"

"True," the woman, said quietly.

A heavy silence hung between them then, until Danny spoke again.

"I had a wife," he explained, "and I almost had a baby daughter. The birth didn't go too well, you know." Danny paused for a moment, and when he went on, his voice was different, as though something had lodged in his throat.

"I just think that if I see that light, just once, even, I'll know that they've gone on to something else. I'd like to know that."

He ran his hands roughly through his hair, more for the purpose of wiping his sleeves past his suddenly wet cheeks. If the woman saw, she kindly pretended not to.

"I could tell you that your wife and daughter are eternal," she said gently, "but I know that you won't believe it until you see some proof. So I'll leave you now and let you do your searching." She stood up and brushed away the dried grass that clung to her dress.

Danny rose, too, and smiled gratefully at the woman.

"Well, thanks," he said, awkwardly. "It was nice to tell someone."

The woman smiled and nodded with understanding. Then she turned to leave.

"Goodbye 'Tom Munson's wife,' " Danny said.

The woman looked back and smiled.

"My name was Annabel," she said, then turned and walked away.

Danny grinned at her mistake.

"And what is it now?" he called after her, but there was no answer. In a matter of three steps, the woman had been enveloped by the darkness.

Danny felt weary then and certain that the ghost light would never show up on such a crowded night. He decided to start out for home and turned to pick up the neatly wrapped leftover sandwich that he had set on the ground when he rose to bid the woman goodbye. As he did, another noisy car turned onto the shoulder of the road to park, splashing its headlights briefly across the tombstone as it did.

And, then, Danny understood why Tom Munson's name had sounded familiar.

During his many visits to the cemetery, Danny had read each of the weathered tombstones at least once. The one against which he had been leaning stood out for its spare, undetailed epitaph.

"Here Lies Thomas Munson," read the first two lines. Below that, almost as an afterthought, were the words "and his Wife."

His wife.

Danny spun around, scanning the dark, little cemetery for Annabel Munson. She was not there. He looked for rustling bushes, a sign that someone was cutting through to the road or the fields beyond. There was no movement.

"Annabel?" he called out. There was no answer.

Danny Pierce sat down on the dry, grassy ground beside the Munsons' grave. He stayed there for several minutes, clutching his forgotten sandwich and replaying the events of the previous minutes in his mind.

Eventually, because there was nothing else to do, he went home.

Several days later, in Esterhazy, he read a headline on the front page of the *Regina Leader-Post.*

"Dozens Witness Tabor Spook Light!" it read.

Danny was usually willing to shell out a few pennies for a copy of a paper with such a headline, but this time, he walked away.

He walked away whistling, in fact. The ghost light was an interesting thing, to be sure, but Danny Pierce no longer needed to see it in order to believe.

The Tabor Light is one of the most well-known, and well-documented, ghost lights in Canada. It is a flickering, reddish-hued ball of fire that has frequently been seen along the road that runs past Tabor Cemetery near Esterhazy, Saskatchewan.

Though the phenomenon has been witnessed intermittently since 1905, the light seemed to be the most active, and achieved its greatest popularity, in the latter part of the Depression. During that time, there would be evenings when as many as 100 people would gather along the road by the little cemetery, hoping to view the light or discover its source.

Some drove from as far away as Manitoba and Ontario, a testament to the far-reaching appeal of Tabor Cemetery's seemingly unsolvable mystery.

Of those who visited the cemetery, likely few knew the story of its origin. It was founded in 1903 by a small group of Bohemian settlers who had become openly atheistic. They chose for their burial ground this desolate site, miles from any church, so that no clergymen could oversee their funerals.

Many of the older headstones in Tabor Cemetery reflect the unceremonious approach to burial that these people held. Few honor their dead with elaborate or poetic phrases, and some fail to remember them even by name.

Case in point, there truly is one simple stone which marks the double grave of a particular man and the woman who is acknowledged only as "his wife."

The Motel

Glenn got home from work an hour late on that Friday. Erica had sandwiches made and bags packed, but it still took 30 minutes more to leave the house. Then there was the traffic, a complicated snarl that held them as slow-moving hostages until they had cleared the city limits. The delays stacked up, one by one, until it was past eight o'clock before the couple's car was heading north on Highway 11.

"We're going to be so late," complained Erica. "We should have just called them and said that we'd drive up in the morning."

"Will you relax?" said Glenn, who held a white-knuckle death grip on the steering wheel. "We'll get there in good time. Everything'll be fine."

He spent the next hour swearing at slow drivers who wouldn't pull over to let him pass and bemoaning the utter recklessness of those who passed him.

After Gravenhurst, the traffic thinned out a little. After Bracebridge, it thinned out a lot. Rain had begun to come down, more in waves than in drops, and sensible drivers had pulled off the road.

"I can't see a thing," said Erica. "How can you drive in this?"

"It's fine," said Glenn. His nose was nearly touching the windshield, and he squinted into the darkness. The wipers were working at their highest velocity, slapping water away from the glass. They couldn't work fast enough though; the few things that were ineffectively illuminated by the headlights appeared to be swimming.

"I think we should stop," said Erica, and she pulled out a map to search for a suitable location.

"We're not stopping! We can't be more than half an hour away!" yelled Glenn. "Doug's doing steaks! We're going to have beers out on the dock!"

"At this time of night?" Erica shouted, in return. "In *this?* You're hallucinating, Glenn!"

They saw the sign then, a bright neon oval by the side of the road. *MOTEL*, it read, in reddish-orange capital letters. Beneath that, in blinking blue script that was missing a tooth, Glenn and Erica saw the word *vac ncy*.

Glenn, who was developing a blinding headache from the near-zero visibility and was exhausted from a long day's work, recognized an opportunity.

"Fine!" he hissed at Erica. "You want to stop, we'll stop. You want to disappoint our friends, that's no problem. Here we go. I hope you're happy."

He hit the brakes and took a hard right turn onto the unpaved turnoff beneath the sign.

"It doesn't look very—occupied," Erica said as they neared the motel's little stand-alone office. Even in the dark and the rain, it was obvious that the building was in need of repair. A torn window screen flapped in the wind, and of the cluster of three naked light bulbs that were affixed to the wall above the front door, two had burned out.

"It's a little late to be changing your mind," Glenn fumed, as he parked beneath the small carport. He jumped out quickly and strode toward the door. He wanted to register before Erica *could* change her mind.

The screen door issued a rusty groan as Glenn opened it and walked into the office. It made twice as much noise when its metal spring pulled it shut. Still, no one emerged from the inside door that Glenn assumed led to some small living quarters.

He cleared his throat loudly and scuffed his shoes purposely, as he crossed the dirty, scarred, tile floor. With the palm of his hand Glenn hit the small silver bell sitting on the scratched countertop. As the echoing ring slowly died away, the only other sound to be heard was the drone of a mosquito flitting about near the ceiling light.

Glenn was about to strike the bell again when he noticed the yellowing, handwritten sign that had been laid flat on the counter, right by the two smooth spots that had been worn away where countless pairs of elbows had rested over the decades. "Welcome" had been written across the top of the heavy paper. "Pls. leave $10 in envelope and take key" it read below that.

"Pretty trusting out here in cottage country," Glenn mumbled to himself as he pulled two five-dollar bills out of his wallet. "Pretty cheap, too." He took the only room key that remained on the wall rack and went back out to the car.

"We're looking for unit number 13," he told Erica, as he put the car in gear.

"I didn't see anyone come into the office with you," she said.

"It's sort of an honor system," he explained.

The car crept along in front of a line of motel rooms that stood as dark as tombs. After a few seconds, the headlights splashed across the number 13.

"Here we go," said Glenn.

Before they got out of the car, Glenn handed Erica the room key.

"You run and open the door," he said, "and I'll get our stuff out of the trunk. No sense in us both getting soaked."

Erica squinted to see past the rivulets of water that ran down the windshield.

"Don't need the key," she said. "The door's already open."

Glenn saw that she was right.

That's strange, he thought to himself, as he pulled the suitcases from the trunk. *An open door is supposed to feel welcoming.*

But it didn't, in this case. It didn't at all.

Ten minutes later, Glenn was still watching the rain pour down. Instead of staring through the car's tinted windshield, though, he was standing on a patch of threadbare carpet, peering out the motel room window at the vast, dark parking lot.

"You know, there's not a single other vehicle here," he said to Erica, who was drying her hands on a t-shirt.

"Is that surprising?" she said, in an irritated tone. "Who the hell would want to stay in a place that doesn't even put *towels* in the rooms! I'm willing to bet that there won't be any sheets on the beds, either."

"You wanted to stop," Glenn shrugged.

"I didn't ask to stop *here*," Erica threw back at him.

They were quiet for a few moments then, and Glenn felt Erica move up behind him. Her breath was warm on his shoulder as she gazed out over the deserted lot.

"The thing I can't figure out is since no one's here, where were the other keys?" Glenn said to her.

"What did you say?" Erica called out.

Glenn spun around. His wife was in the bathroom.

"What are you doing there?" he said, and his voice betrayed his shock.

"Taking off my makeup. What's wrong with *you?*" Erica said, as she looked him up and down.

I'm tired. I'm just tired, he thought, as his heart slowed to its normal rhythm. Out loud, he said, "Nothing's wrong with me, except that we would have been at Doug and Sandy's place by now if we hadn't stopped."

"Or in the ditch," shot Erica, and returned to the bathroom.

Glenn was too weary to think of a snappy response and decided to simply go to bed. He sat down on the sagging mattress and pulled off his socks.

He turned around twice while he did it, certain that Erica had quietly joined him. Each time, he saw that she was still in the bathroom.

I've got a case of the willies, he thought, remembering the expression from his boyhood. *The heebie-jeebies, the scarios, the creature-feature creeps.* He found that he couldn't keep himself from rubbing the back of his neck, so persistent was the feeling that strange eyes were focused upon him there.

"You know," he called out to Erica, trying to fill the room with conversation, "when we drove up here last year, I didn't notice this place."

"Me neither," she said. "Although, it would have been pretty easy to miss if it hadn't been for that sign. Maybe the sign is new."

"Hmm," said Glenn. "It didn't look new."

Glenn found himself aching for sleep. As he sat on the edge of the creaking queen-size bed, he longed to put his

head down on the flat pillow and close his eyes. He wanted
to pull the stale-smelling blankets up over his shoulder and
listen to the rain beating down on the roof and turn his
anxious mind off until morning when he would wake and
be able to laugh at the eerie thoughts that had haunted him
the night before.

Get undressed, he instructed himself. *Go to sleep. Stop
being an idiot.*

And then he tried to take his shirt off.

The instant his skin was bared, it began to crawl.

What do you know? That's not just an expression, some
detached part of his mind marveled. And it was true. The
tiny hairs that covered his body were standing at attention;
gooseflesh had begun to rise, and Glenn's skin was actually
starting to creep into a taut sort of alertness.

The sensation of eyes upon him was that overwhelming.

Glenn's breath began to come in short, rapid hitches. He
pulled his shirt tightly around him and scanned the room for
intruders. He could see no one. He could sense someone.
Maybe even many someones, for the feeling of being watched
was growing. An accompanying dread grew within Glenn.

If I go to sleep, here, something terrible will happen.

He knew it, as surely as he knew his name.

Glenn was sitting there, hyperventilating, with sour panic
churning in his gut, when Erica walked out of the bathroom.

"You know there's no curtain on that little window, above
the shower?" she griped. "Sure, it's high up, but if someone
wanted to, they could have a pretty good view in there."

Glenn jumped off the bed.

"That's it!" he said, and his voice was shaking. "All you've
done is bitch about this place, and now you're waiting for

Norman Bates to do his Peeping Tom act! We're leaving, Erica. Get your stuff together. We're going!"

Glenn stuffed his feet into his shoes and didn't bother to tie the laces. He grabbed the suitcases and the few items that had been unpacked and threw open the motel room door.

"Hurry up!" he screamed at Erica. He was feeling more desperate by the minute, more certain that if they didn't leave immediately, they would never leave at all.

Erica gathered her things without saying a word. Glenn's outburst shocked her into obeying, although his behavior seemed irrational.

Once they were in the car and speeding away from the little motel, she cast a critical eye over her husband.

"You've got a screw loose, Glenn," she finally said.

And deep down, he worried that she was right.

The next day, once Doug and Sandy had gotten over their irritation at having been awakened by rain-soaked guests in the middle of the night, Glenn sought his friend out for a bit of conversation.

"You're up here every weekend," he said, "so you must be familiar with that little motel. The one on the east side of the highway, just south of Huntsville."

"South of Huntsville," mused Doug. "There's no motel there."

"Sure, there is," insisted Glenn, and went on to describe the place in detail.

After a few minutes, a look of recognition flashed across Doug's face.

"Okay, okay," he said. "I know the one you mean. So what about it?"

Glenn didn't know exactly what to ask, so he finally said, "Do they do much business?"

"Business?" asked Doug, and he looked confused, again.

Glenn decided to try a different angle. "Did you and Sandy ever stay there?"

"How could we have?" Doug replied, and he looked at Glenn with an odd expression. "I didn't know Sandy then."

"You didn't know Sandy when?" It was Glenn's turn to appear confused.

"Before they tore the place down. I remember it was 1977, because I was 16. I'd just gotten my driver's license, and I went out there with a buddy to watch the big neon sign come down. It was a god-awful thing; the second 'a' in 'vacancy' burned out about the time the Beatles broke up, and they never fixed it," he concluded.

The remainder of the weekend seemed agonizingly long to Glenn.

"Why do you want to leave so early?" Erica groused as they drove away from their friends' cottage immediately after Sunday brunch.

"Beat the traffic," was all Glenn said, but something about the way he said it made Erica drop the topic.

As they began to drive south on Highway 11, Erica sensed a difference in Glenn. He was driving slowly, letting the stream of traffic flow past them.

"What the hell are you looking for?" she finally said, after he had checked the rearview mirror for the hundredth time.

Glenn sighed. "Nothing," he said, and it wasn't a lie. There was nothing there to look for, nothing to be found; he was convinced of it. He had scanned every roadside inch since they had driven out of Huntsville and found no sign of the motel. His eyes hurt and his mind hurt, and there was a knot of raw fear in the pit of his stomach.

"I'm not looking for anything," he assured Erica, and stepped on the gas. Within seconds, the car was on the tail of the vehicle ahead of it, and Glenn pulled out to pass. Before he cut back into traffic, he glanced briefly in the rearview mirror.

And there it was.

Afternoon thunderclouds had begun to gather in the north. Against that bruised, threatening backdrop, the big oval neon sign stood like a beacon.

Vac ncy, it flashed. *Vac ncy*. A welcome invitation to weary tourists about to be caught in a summer storm.

It was there for a second, and then it was gone. Glenn was left gaping into the mirror.

"Would you mind watching the road, just a little?" Erica carped when the driver behind them blasted his horn. Glenn rubbed his eyes wearily.

"I *am* watching the road," he snapped. "It's right where it's supposed to be."

Glenn risked only one more backward glance. He saw nothing that should not have been there. Wanting to keep it that way, he turned up the radio and put his foot down and checked the rearview as infrequently as possible from that point on.

As he had predicted, they beat the traffic and made it back to the city in record time.

This tale is a variation on a story that was recounted by a fellow author who has interviewed countless subjects regarding their personal experiences with the paranormal.

It stands out as unique among ghost stories, being a rare example of a haunting in which the location is the actual ghost.

Mother's Day

On the morning of May 15, Claire looked at her kitchen calendar and admitted defeat. It was Tuesday. Mother's Day was Sunday. For the third year running, she would have to send her mother something expensive and impersonal, instead of the thoughtful gift that she had planned.

"Flowers or gourmet basket?" she asked herself wearily and dropped the yellow pages on the countertop with a dull *whump*.

She ended up ordering a bouquet of spring flowers in a whimsical ceramic vase shaped like a teapot. The card would be signed *Love, Claire*, in someone else's handwriting.

After Claire hung up the phone, she picked up the big plastic craft box that had been sitting on her kitchen table for three weeks. She had put it there deliberately, where it was inconvenient and obvious, and she would be forced to look at it daily. She felt that if she had to eat her meals with it, she would eventually have to deal with it. She had been wrong. Claire had discovered that she was usually capable of ignoring the box entirely, and on days when it did bother her conscience, she simply ate in the living room, or upstairs at her desk, or while sitting on one of the tall stools by the counter. But the game was officially over for another year, and the box went back into the smallest upstairs bedroom where Claire kept her exercise bike and her wedding photos and other things of which she did not wish to be reminded.

The box was filled with photographs and other special mother-daughter mementos, which Claire planned to someday arrange creatively in an expensive scrapbook with a hand-painted cover. There was an abundance of project supplies in the box as well: a dozen pairs of special edging scissors, several books of patterned, acid-free background paper, stencils and colored pens. Often, Claire would buy some new materials for the scrapbook—a pen that wrote in silver-colored ink, a cellophane package of die-cut photo borders—but she never actually did anything with them. Birthdays, Christmases and now three Mother's Days had come and gone, and the gift had not been given. As Claire hoisted the box onto the top shelf of the bedroom's tiny closet, she consoled herself with the knowledge that, that year, she had more than the usual number of excuses.

Her marriage had ended. She had left Chicago. She'd bought a house that needed renovating. And, Claire was working more than ever.

As a freelance writer whose income waxed and waned according to the number of assignments that came in, Claire couldn't complain about that. Still, she had come to feel that she was spending her life on the brink of one looming deadline after another, with no breathing space between. The one lull that she might have enjoyed had been filled to capacity when her friend Fay had phoned her one day and said, "Feel like taking a drive? I've got a great deal for you on a lovely, old, painted lady."

Fay was a real-estate agent who knew of Claire's love for historic homes. Her office was in Woodstock—a nest of Victorian charm an hour north of the city—and she made a point of keeping her eyes open for Claire. Not that Claire had requested it. She wasn't even sure that she wanted to leave Chicago.

"What about work?" she had said, as she wandered through the sunny rooms of the old, empty house.

"What about it?" had been Fay's reply. "You think you can't put a fax machine here? You think we don't have Internet access? How many face-to-face meetings do you actually take?"

Fay had shown Claire the attic then and explained how easily it would convert into a home office. In the end, because Claire couldn't think of a good reason not to, she bought the fading house with its gingerbread trim and creaking hardwood floors and left her old life 65 miles behind her.

She moved in one gray day in March, when the bare-branched trees looked like a protective sentry guarding the perimeter of the old building.

The house, of course, needed work. There was painting to be done and floors to be refinished and plaster cracks to be mended. On the first evening, Claire had lit candles and opened a bottle of zinfandel and wandered around her new home with half-closed eyes, trying to imagine what it would look like when the moving crates were unpacked and everything was repaired.

"I love you," she said to the house, because she was a little giddy from exhaustion and wine. "I'm going to make you beautiful again."

She had been in the dining room then, picturing new wallpaper above the lovely dark wainscoting and thinking that she would scour the antique shops for some china to display on the plate rails. The candles were casting their soft light, and Claire sipped her drink, took off her glasses and deliberately blurred her vision, making the room look as warm and romantic as possible. She was feeling more content, hopeful and happy than she had in months. She was relaxed, basking in the good feelings, when she detected some motion in the periphery of her vision. A dark shape, like a concentrated shadow, slipped soundlessly past the arched door that opened into the hall. It was enough to make Claire jump, and a little wine slopped out of her glass. Almost immediately though, she had dismissed it.

Drinking on an empty stomach; serves you right, she scolded herself, before she went looking for something to wipe at the wet patch on her t-shirt. After a moment, she decided to simply exchange the light top for something long-sleeved and warm. She had been comfortable earlier, but suddenly there was a chill that was raising gooseflesh on her arms.

Two weeks later, as Claire sat in her new attic office enjoying the spring sunshine that poured through the window, she was visited by another sly blanket of cold.

She had been rewriting the sidebars for an article due the following day and eating wheat crackers smeared with strawberry jam and wondering if she should cut her hair short for the summer. She had been interrupted quite suddenly on all levels by an unfamiliar voice.

Alice.

Later, Claire found it difficult to say whether the word was spoken aloud or somehow projected into her mind. It had surprised her, though, and all the humming static of her normal functioning state came to an abrupt halt.

"What?..." she had said, before remembering that she was completely alone. Claire turned away from her laptop then and glanced nervously around the sprawling attic. No one was there. Nothing was out of place. All was quiet.

Then that quiet was punctured by a sudden creaking that made Claire suck her breath in sharply. She let it out in a relieved sigh when she saw that it was only the poorly balanced door to the stairs. Claire preferred to keep it shut, but the stubborn thing frequently swung open and had done so again. As she walked over to close it, she decided that she would first run down to her bedroom and grab a sweater. The attic had been stuffy and warm earlier in the morning, but the sudden *breeze* (Claire described it to herself that way, although the air had not exactly moved) had the fine hair on her arms and neck all standing straight up from the cold.

Claire ran lightly down the narrow staircase that led from the attic to the second floor. She moved quickly and rubbed her arms vigorously as she went, but the movement did little to warm her. By the time she had reached her bedroom and pulled open a dresser drawer, her teeth were nearly chattering with the cold.

She spotted an old favorite, stuffed in the bottom of one drawer: a badly stretched and paint-splattered gray sweatshirt that hung halfway down her thighs. "Ahhh," she breathed with satisfaction as she pulled the soft fleecy garment over her head.

Alice.

The word was spoken as the sweatshirt slid past Claire's ears. She froze, with folds of soft gray fleece bunched in her armpits.

"Who's there?" she whispered. The house thrummed with silence.

Slowly and quietly, Claire pulled the sweatshirt down over her body. She hugged its thick, warm fabric around her but couldn't stop shivering. She walked out of the bedroom, one silent step at a time, and stood, listening, in the hallway. Around the corner, by the small bedroom, where she could not see, a floorboard creaked loudly.

"Oh, grow up, Claire," she said, more loudly, in an attempt to banish her fear. "You've always wanted to live in an old house, and now you're going to jump every time the floor squeaks?"

There was another sound then—not a floorboard but the dull, yawning groan of door hinges. It, too, came from the small bedroom. Claire's heart pounded. She wanted badly to run down the broad main staircase and out the front entrance, into the pale spring sunshine. Instead, she forced herself to turn the corner in the hall and walk back to the bedroom that she had been using for nothing but storage.

There were no furnishings in the room, and no curtains had been hung on the one narrow window. Cardboard cartons and a miscellany of unused items were stacked against the walls. Claire knew that those things occupied the small bedroom. She saw none of them when she stepped through the doorway.

The window, directly opposite the door, was what shocked her first. It was bordered by panels of filmy floral fabric, with a valence of similar material that covered the workings of a beige, fringed, roll blind. Beyond the glass, the blue spring sky had turned the color of gunmetal, and a few small snowflakes twirled lazily on their downward voyage.

Claire's jaw dropped. Her knees became unreliable, and she groped blindly for some form of support. Her hand connected with an unfamiliar surface, and she looked down to find that she was leaning on a mahogany dressing table that she had never before seen. A lace runner covered the top of it, and on that lay a neat assortment of tortoiseshell combs and brushes. The attached mirror reflected the other furnishings in the room: a matching mahogany half tester bed covered with layers of ivory lace and plump feather pillows, a fussy upholstered chair and a little painted table, which held a dainty dollhouse and a number of carefully displayed toys. Narrow shelves marked the point where the varnished wainscoting gave way to delicately patterned wallpaper, and a collection of small china figurines stood quietly at attention upon them.

Oh, my Alice!...

Claire reeled around in shock. It was the same voice she had heard in the attic and in her bedroom, but more powerful. Not louder, exactly, but infused with more emotion. It was a woman speaking—Claire was surprised to note that she had only just become certain of that—and the woman was in absolute anguish.

"Where are you?" Claire called out. "What's the matter?"

A large column of air beside the bed began to shimmer. A shadow formed within it, and some dark shape began to coalesce there. There was a distant, tinny, ringing sound.

And then it all vanished.

Claire found herself sitting on the floor, looking at the haphazard stacks of her junk. The bulky sweatshirt was bunched up around her shoulder blades, which told her that she had slid down the wall before landing on her bum. She had no memory of it, though. Conversely, there was no evidence of the things that she did remember from the previous few minutes. Only the insistent ringing continued, and, after a moment, Claire recognized it to be the telephone.

"Hello?"

Claire answered the phone in her bedroom, but it had still taken a good 10 rings before she reached it. On the other end was Fay, who was having such a slow afternoon that she had been content to wait.

"Hi neighbor!" Fay chirped, and Claire could picture her at her desk, doodling contentedly on one of the specially made notepads that read *Fay Halsey Holds the Key to Your Happy Home.* There was a smiling caricature of Fay-the-happy-realtor in the upper right hand corner, dangling an oversized key from one finger.

"Did you sell me a haunted house?" Claire blurted. There followed a long, heavy moment of silence.

Finally, Fay spoke. "Claire—why would you ask me that?" she said, and she no longer sounded bright and doodling.

"Can you just tell me?" Claire pleaded. "I'm not—*accusing* you of anything. I just need to know. Did you ever hear any stories about this place? Did anything weird ever happen to the last owners?" She grimaced silently and covered her face with one hand. *I sound crazy* she thought, as she waited for Fay's reply.

Fay answered slowly and thoughtfully and if she thought that Claire sounded crazy, she hid it well.

"I never heard a ghost story about your house," she said, with such sincerity that Claire believed her. Fay was quiet for a moment then and seemed to be working up to something. "There is sort of—an *unsavory* story about the place," she finally admitted. Claire held her breath and waited for her friend to continue.

"Something like a hundred years ago, a woman committed suicide in your house," Fay explained. "She was looking after her daughter; the kid was dying of cholera, or something, and the mother wanted to die with her. She drank poison. It worked. She died." Fay sighed then and offered something of an apology.

"I wasn't keeping it from you, Claire," she said. "I honestly just didn't think to tell you. It happened a long time ago. The only reason I even know is because of that local history nut that used to answer the phones here."

"What was her name?" Claire asked, suddenly.

"Oh, it was Lucy something-or-other. I could check my payroll records..."

"No, no," snapped Claire. "I mean the woman who *died* here."

"Oh, of course," said Fay. "It was, um, Mary. Mary Lundgren."

Claire was disappointed for only a moment, before the facts came together for her.

"And her daughter's name was Alice!" she said.

"Yeah, you're right!" said Fay, and she sounded impressed. "How did you know?"

Then, over the course of the next half hour, Claire told her.

In the weeks that followed, Claire came to accept that she was living with a ghost. When she was painting the parlor a lovely, rich shade of burgundy and her fine edging brush kept disappearing, she blamed Mary Lundgren.

When she sat at her desk and felt a sudden shock of cold air settle on the back of her neck, she assumed that Mary was visiting. Once, she had watched a shimmering patch of air, like a heat wave, ascend the main staircase, while the steps beneath the shape creaked, one by one. Another time, while soaking in the old clawfoot tub, Claire had heard the intermittent sound of a woman humming. It had been like listening to a radio that was not quite tuned to the frequency. As Claire marveled at the sound, the steaming bath water went instantly cold around her.

Despite all of that, it took only a couple of uneventful weeks to make Claire doubt her memory of all that she had experienced in the house. By the time she ordered the flowers for her mother, she had begun to convince herself that it had been a strange, waking dream.

"I was under such stress," she told Fay, later that day, over garlicky Caesar salads at one of the town's trendy little eateries. "I'd just moved. I signed the papers for the divorce and the papers for the house something like five weeks apart. My desk was piled with work. I think I just took a little mental vacation, or something. What do you think?"

"I think that I should have ordered something a little more breath-friendly, considering I have to show two houses this afternoon," Fay replied, then sighed and set down her fork. "I don't know. I just don't know about that kind of stuff. Have you asked anyone else?"

"You're the only friend I have in Woodstock," said Claire. "Actually, you were my only friend even before I moved to Woodstock, so there is no second opinion to be had."

"You've had some weird things happening," said Fay. She had stopped eating her salad and was chewing on the parsley garnish from her bread plate. She made a mental note to buy gum on her way back to the office.

"I know," said Claire. "But so much of it could be the power of suggestion, don't you think? I mean—I wig out and have what is admittedly a very strange experience. As a result of that, I learn about Mary Lundgren's suicide. I have to wonder if everything that's happened since then isn't just because I've been expecting it to happen. Do you know what I mean?"

Fay nodded thoughtfully.

"But how did you know the little girl's name?" she asked Claire.

There was a long pause while Claire thought about it. Finally, she shrugged and stabbed her fork into a crouton.

"I don't know," was all she said.

That night, after calling the florist and hiding away the craft box and having the conversation with Fay, Claire went to bed thinking about her mother and Alice Lundgren's mother. As she began to float into lucid dreaming, she imagined that they had merged into one long-suffering woman.

"I'm sorry about the flowers," Claire mumbled, as she slipped further away from consciousness. "You've been waiting for that book for a hundred years..." There was no answer. There was nothing then but darkness and when Claire looked at the clock again, several hours had passed.

Alice!

It was Mary Lundgren's voice that woke her, and it sounded more desperate and mournful than usual. Claire rubbed her eyes and sat up in bed. She looked over at the bedroom door just in time to see a dusky silhouette slip past in the hall.

Alice, I'm coming, darling.

Claire swung her feet out from beneath the covers. *I have to talk to Mary,* she thought, groggily. *Alice is sick, and she doesn't have her Mother's Day present ready.*

Claire padded down the hallway in her bare feet, following the sounds of other footsteps that were making their way toward the small, back bedroom. Someone there was weeping; Claire could hear the soft, hiccuping sobs even before she rounded the corner in the hall. When she walked into the little room, the feeling of distress was oppressive.

The tasteful, carefully arranged things that Claire had seen once before were now in a state of disarray. The tortoiseshell hairdressing set had been swept off the dresser to the floor. In its place were several dark glass bottles bearing pharmacy labels, and a large pitcher of water. The dollhouse and other toys had been piled haphazardly in one corner, so that the little table could hold a basin and a pile of flannel cloths. The bedcovers were in a crumpled pile near the footboard and appeared to be soiled. The stench of sweat and diarrhea and sickness pervaded the room.

There was no one to be seen, but the sobbing had grown louder. Claire's heart ached sympathetically.

"Mary, I want to help you," she whispered.

And then she screamed.

Inches from her own face, the haggard, wretched features of another woman had instantly materialized.

"She's dying!" the woman screamed, and her eyes bulged with wild, pure fear. "She's dying, my little Alice, and I can't bear it! Look at her!"

Claire was frantically backing away from the raving phantom of Mary Lundgren but did manage to steal a look at Alice's sickbed. It remained rumpled, reeking and empty. The ghost, however, seemed to see something there. She hurried back to the bedside and stooped over it, weeping. Her hands moved above the stinking sheets, as though caressing some invisible shape.

"Alice! Don't be afraid, Alice. I won't let you go alone," she cried.

Then, suddenly, her hysterical focus returned to Claire. In one supernaturally fluid flash of movement, the wraith stood nose to nose with her again. Her face was etched with pain, and permanent, blue hollows hung beneath her wild, darting eyes. Her sour breath invaded Claire's nostrils.

"Get me the bottle from under the sink," she rasped.

And Claire woke up.

She was gasping for air, and her nose was plugged with mucus. When she opened her eyes, fresh tears spilled over her already wet cheeks. Her heart thudded against her ribs, and her hands, which had been clenched into tight fists against her body, began to tingle as she released her fingers and blood flowed back into them. As consciousness took a firmer hold of her and she began to realize that it had all been a dream, relief washed over her in sweet waves.

"Thank God," Claire moaned as she pulled the tassel cord on the bedside lamp. "Thank God, thank God..." she repeated as warm, comforting light filled the room.

She had to blow her nose and wait several minutes before she felt steady enough to walk to the bathroom. Once there, she turned on the cold water tap and splashed several handfuls on her face. The shock of it was good, and she remained bent over the sink for a while, letting the water drip off her nose and chin. Claire focused on taking deep, calming breaths. When she felt centered again, she stood up in front of the mirrored medicine chest and reached for a towel.

Her reflection showed the drawn, ghastly face of Mary Lundgren peering over her shoulder.

"Did you find the bottle?" Mary said, just before Claire fainted.

Twenty minutes later, Claire had every light in the house blazing brightly and was holding an ice pack to the swelling spot where she had hit her head on the bathroom's hard, tile floor. It was 3:30 in the morning, she was standing in the middle of her kitchen, and she had just dialed Fay's home number. When her friend answered in the sleepy, worried tone appropriate for calls received in the wee hours, Claire didn't even take the time to say hello.

"Get over here, Fay!" she nearly screamed, into the phone. "Please, right now, come over!"

Fay arrived in 12 minutes flat, wearing her bathrobe and carrying a half bottle of brandy.

By the time the sky had begun to show its pale morning colors, the brandy and two pots of coffee had been consumed. Claire and Fay sat together at the kitchen table, having a conversation in raw, disconnected bursts.

"We'll list the house," Fay said, at one point. "I won't take a commission—maybe you can get your money back."

"I can't move again. Not now," Claire shook her head. A few minutes later, she said, "Maybe an exorcist?"

"I wouldn't know where to find one, would you?" asked Fay.

There was a long period of silence then. Finally, Claire sighed, stood up and took the two empty mugs over to the sink. She appeared lost in thought and spent a long time rinsing the coffee dregs down the drain. Finally, she shook her head.

"You know what's strange, Fay?" she asked.

Fay's eyebrows arched in a cynical expression.

"Something's strange, here?" she said. "Give me a moment, maybe I can figure it out."

"No, really," said Claire. "I think it's odd—considering the whole story, that is—I think it's odd that little Alice's ghost isn't here, too. I mean, I don't think she is. I never sense her."

Fay looked confused.

"Well, why would you? She didn't die. I mean, you know, not until a few years ago. I remember Lucy talking about it. You remember—'Miss Historical Society.' "

Claire turned and stared stupidly at Fay.

"She didn't *die?*"

"No," Fay shook her head vigorously. "I mean, that was the thing, about it, right? The mother was so distraught about her daughter's imminent demise that she took poison, and then the kid pulled through. Kick in the pants, huh? I guess I forgot to tell you that part..." she trailed off, weakly.

"Oh, God, and she never knew. She *doesn't* know!" Claire's hands flew to her face, in an expression of horrible understanding. Suddenly, it had begun to make sense. Mary was trapped in her terrible, final moments. For a century, she had suffered, not knowing that things had turned out differently than expected for Alice.

Claire looked at the kitchen calendar then and knew what she had to do.

"I have four days," she whispered.

"What?" Fay had put her head down on the table and looked ready to doze off.

"Four days!" said Claire, suddenly animated, suddenly alive with purpose. "And I need your help, Fay. You have to help me." She grabbed one of Fay's own Happy Realtor notepads from the clutter of things that occupied the top of the fridge and then rummaged in the kitchen junk drawer for a pen. She put both on the table in front of her sleepy, bewildered friend.

"I have to go take a shower," Claire explained, "and while I'm gone, I want you to write down everything you know about Alice Lundgren. Everything!"

Then Claire was gone, taking the stairs two at a time, and Fay was left looking at her own smiling caricature.

"Everything I know, huh?" she mumbled to herself. "Good thing these pads are small."

Claire spent most of that morning on the phone.

The first call had been to the editor of a small travel magazine that was expecting her article on European cycling tours the following Monday. Claire held a wad of tissue over the mouthpiece as she spoke, told a bald-faced lie about having come down with the flu and bought herself a one-week extension.

She accepted the editor's sympathies with a small pang of guilt, then hung up, tossed the tissue in the garbage, cleared her throat and dialed city hall.

"I need to speak to someone in the public records office," she said.

After city hall, there was the library. After the library, there was the newspaper. And after Claire had talked to a bored-sounding part-time clerk in the newspaper archives, she called Fay, whom she had sent to work with only a few hours' sleep, a full-blown brandy hangover and a list of non-work-related tasks to accomplish.

"Well?" she asked.

"Well, I talked to her," Fay said, then yawned hugely. "She said tomorrow's good. She'll be at home pasting obituaries onto Bristol board, or whatever it is those people do."

Claire took down the address and phone number.

"And it's 'Lucy,' right?" she asked Fay.

"Right," said Fay. "Lucy Bartlett. You realize, of course, that I have a lunch date with her, now. I have to spend an hour, next Wednesday, hearing about stunning advancements in the world of genealogy."

"Your sacrifice is duly noted," Claire assured her, then hung up.

Lucy Bartlett turned out to be a smartly dressed woman in her forties who was neither obsessive nor dull, as Fay's sarcastic comments had suggested. She offered Claire iced tea, and they sat together on a tidy little patio where Claire provided a judiciously edited version of her story.

"So, for me, part of restoring the house is learning about the lives of those who lived there," she told Lucy. It wasn't *exactly* a lie.

"And you want to begin with Alice Lundgren," Lucy nodded. "Well, that's logical."

"It is?" Claire was surprised. She had anticipated having to make up some story to explain why she was starting her research in the middle of the house's history.

"Well, yes. Alice was very involved in the community, all her life. You'll have an easier time finding material about her than you would about any other member of her family," Lucy explained.

It was exactly what Claire wanted to hear. She set her glass on the little wrought-iron table next to her chair and leaned forward eagerly.

"So where do I start?" she asked.

Lucy Bartlett gave Claire a list of suggestions. She told her where to find the best collection of microfilm and which office held the city directories that were more than 50 years old. She knew which cemetery Alice Lundgren was buried in and even produced a copy of a beautifully printed memorial program from her funeral. Claire was impressed and told Lucy so.

"If I ever need a researcher, I'll know where to look," she said. Lucy had laughed.

"I'm afraid I'm only this resourceful when it comes to my own little corner of the world," she said. "Outside of Woodstock, I'm useless."

Lucy Bartlett had walked Claire out to her car then, and the two women said their goodbyes. Lucy was about to walk back through her front gate when something made her pause. She turned back to Claire, and there was curiosity written on her face.

"Listen," she said, and her tone was confidential, "it's absolutely none of my business, but I have to ask you something." She paused, as if waiting for permission.

"Go on," said Claire.

"It's about your house," Lucy said. "I've heard...well, I've heard that it's haunted. Is there any truth to that?"

Claire laughed aloud, for the first time in days. "Let's just say that I should have talked to you before I bought it," she said, then drove away.

By Saturday afternoon, Claire had a legal-sized manila envelope stuffed with blurry newspaper articles, photos, announcements and documents of various natures. She carried it into the little back bedroom, along with a pair of scissors and a roll of cellophane tape.

She had already moved the assortment of boxes out to the hallway. The bedroom had been tidied, and on the bare wall, where the head of Alice's mahogany half tester bed had been, Claire began to create.

It was a shrine, of sorts, that she was making. Claire trimmed and taped and began to decorate the wall with the documentary proof of Alice's existence.

The first item to go up was the announcement of her birth—the happy news that a six-pound baby girl had been born to Mr. and Mrs. Hubert Lundgren. Then there was a copy of the little girl's first grade report. Both had been in a collection of Lundgren family papers that had been donated to the historical society some time in the 1970s.

The item after that made Claire pause. It was a newspaper article detailing Mary Lundgren's suicide and Alice's bout with cholera. After a few moments, Claire ran up to her office and grabbed a yellow highlighting pen. With two bold strokes, she accentuated the final, rambling sentence of the article:

"Mrs. Lundgren's young daughter, who was herself gravely ill in these past several days, is now growing stronger, and is expected to recover fully, though she is sure to mourn the terrible loss of her own dear mother."

Satisfied with the effect, Claire taped the article to the wall.

There were happier mementos to follow. A photograph of a smiling, teenage Alice, accepting an award for scholastic achievement. A copied record of her high school diploma. Claire had been delighted to come across an actual engraved invitation to the young woman's wedding. While her photocopied version didn't capture the quality of the stationery and artwork, it got the information across. With a piece of tape, it went on the wall.

After Alice Lundgren had become Mrs. Alice Lundgren Powers, the joys and sorrows of family life had begun. There were birth announcements—three in all—and then a black-bordered notice with a tiny, weeping angel in the corner. One of those babies had lived for only a few years. As she taped that one to the wall, Claire spoke out loud to Mary.

"She would have known how you felt, Mary," she said. "She would have understood."

There was a series of clippings, then, concerning the lighter business of life: social events, meetings of the garden club and the time Alice's husband ran for town council and lost. Then there were the letters that the elderly Alice took to writing to the local paper—wryly amusing pieces that were published regularly because they offered more insight than the usual complaints about potholes and trash collection service.

Claire worked her way across the wall, creating a time line for the life of Alice Lundgren. Alice had once been a little girl in the very bedroom where Claire sat, one century later, carefully cutting out her obituary. It was the last article to go on the wall, a period at the end of a long and well-written sentence.

But there was something missing.

Claire found that she was only partially satisfied with the end result. She had managed to demonstrate Alice's life, but somehow it wasn't obvious that it had been done for Mary's benefit, as a gift to her.

"I know!" Claire said, suddenly, and she jumped up and pulled her craft box down from the top shelf of the bedroom closet. For the next 20 minutes, she sat on the floor, bent intently over sheets of colored paper with a stencil and a marker. She outlined rows of letters, which she then carefully cut out and taped to the wall above the display.

HAPPY MOTHER'S DAY, the words above the photos and clippings read. Beneath, it read, *LOVE, ALICE.*

Claire was happy then. She swept up the mess of paper cuttings, put away her tools and turned off the light. A few hours later, she drifted easily off to sleep, aided by the gentle sound of falling rain and the peace that had settled within her.

Sometime during the night, Claire was drawn to the surface of her dreamless sleep by a soft sound and a sense of changing atmosphere.

The house just sighed, she thought to herself, and in her twilight state of consciousness, it didn't seem to be a strange thought at all.

Claire woke early on Mother's Day. The rain had stopped, and fresh, cool air was wafting through the bedroom window. Normally, that was something that Claire enjoyed; she liked to make tea on mornings like that and take it back to bed where she would stay contentedly under the covers for as long as time allowed. She didn't want a cup of tea on this morning, though, and she didn't feel the least bit content.

As Claire padded into the bathroom to perform her morning rituals, she thought that she felt lonely. Then she paused for a moment, searching for a more exact explanation.

I feel alone, she amended. That was it. Something, or someone, had been with her for a long time, and Claire was feeling an acute absence of that presence.

She thought of Mary then, and she remembered the gift, and she walked barefoot down the hall to the small bedroom.

The air felt lighter there than it ever had before. Claire was struck with a sense of wonder. *I'll use this room, now*, she thought. It had never before occurred to her that there had been a reason she had avoided it and treated it as a storage closet.

Claire stared at her homemade exhibit, searching for some sign that it had been read or, in some way, taken in. Her eyes roamed to the bottom of the display, and she found her sign there. She began to cry.

The "c" in Alice's name had been turned on its side. Even though the stencil-styled letters were fat and round, the meaning was clear.

It had come to read "Alive."

Later that morning, Claire called her own mother. During the conversation, she shrugged off the gratitude that was offered for her gift.

"They're just flowers, Mom," she said. "I have something else for you—it's just going to be a little late."

When Claire hung up the phone, she brought the craft box downstairs and across her living room floor spread all the things that she had spent years collecting. For a moment, she hesitated. There was so much to do, and she wanted to take the time to do it beautifully.

Then Claire simply picked up one photo, stopped thinking and began to work. For hours, she sat on the floor, pasting pictures and ticket stubs and mementos onto the scrapbook pages. In the margins, she scribbled names and dates and memories. In the end, she ran out of pages before she ran out of time or inspiration.

It wasn't perfect, of course, but it was just right. Claire had finally learned that she was the important part of the gift.

The true story upon which this tale was based is just one of many illustrating that the bond between mother and child is one that cannot be severed by death.

When a child is taken from its mother, no matter what the circumstances, the eventual result is often a maternal spirit who wanders endlessly, in search of her lost little one. Likewise, a mother who passes away when her children are young is likely to return in spirit to watch over them.

True devotion, it would seem, can survive the most extreme separation.